E 812   LBD17/52

KT-214-950

WITHDRAWN

N 0006137 9

ASSESSING ENGLISH

Open University Press

English, Language, and Education series

General Editor: Anthony Adams
Lecturer in Education, University of Cambridge

This series is concerned with all aspects of language in education from the primary school to the tertiary sector. Its authors are experienced educators who examine both principles and practice of English subject teaching and language across the curriculum in the context of current educational and societal developments.

TITLES IN THE SERIES

ASSESSING ENGLISH

Helping Students to Reflect on Their Work

Brian Johnston

while working with

Stephen Dowdy
Sr. Margaret Cain
Marion Burn
and
Helen Richardson

NEWMAN COLLEGE
BARTLEY GREEN
BIRMINGHAM, 32.

CLASS	375.42
ACCESSION	87887
AUTHOR	JOH

Open University Press
Milton Keynes · *Philadelphia*

St Clair Press
Sydney

Open University Press
Open University Educational Enterprises Limited
12 Cofferidge Close
Stony Stratford
Milton Keynes MK11 1BY, England
and
242 Cherry Street
Philadelphia, PA 19106, USA

St. Clair Press,
P. O. Box 314,
Epping, NSW 2121, Australia

First published 1983 by St. Clair Press
This revised edition published jointly 1987 by
Open University Press and St. Clair Press.

© Brian Johnston 1983, 1987.

All rights reserved. No part of this work may be reproduced in any form
by mimeograph or by any other means, without permission in writing
from the publisher.

British Library Cataloguing in Publication Data
Johnston, Brian
  Assessing English : helping students to
  reflect on their work.—Rev. ed.—
  English, Language, and Education series.
  1. English language—Study and teaching
  (secondary)   2. English language—
  Ability testing
  I. Title   II. Series
  420'.7'12   PE1066

ISBN 0–335–15999–0

St. Clair Press   ISBN 0 949898 14 7

Text design by Clarke Williams
Typeset by Marlborough Design, Oxford
Printed in Great Britain by St. Edmundsbury Press, Bury St. Edmunds,
Suffolk.

Contents

Acknowledgements

Some of the material discussed here has appeared in a different form in *English in Australia, The Australian Teacher, Pivot, Curriculum Exchange, Opinion* and *Developments in English Teaching*.

Many people contributed to the work on which this book is based: Stephen Dowdy, Marion Burn, Helen Richardson and Sr Margaret Cain worked, over a long period, to put new ideas into practice in the classroom, even though they knew that only some of their work would eventually be reported in the book.

In addition to the teachers mentioned in the text, the following people made significant contributions: Noel Wilson, Bill Hannan, Nigel Howard, Stephanie Moss, Tanya Rogers, Phil Cormack, Alan Laslett, Anne Hoogendoorn, Tricia Flynn, Rex Rehn, Claire Woods, Paul Tyrrell, Judy Andrews, Judy Peters, Roger Zubrinich, Graham Little, David McRae, Bill Corcoran, Barbara Comber, Brenda Kuhr, Brendan Ryan, Lee Pasco, John McFadyen and Alan Johnston. I was also helped by Cathy Beavis and Garth Boomer, who read and criticized the book while it was being written; and by Rosalie Price, Lyn Wilkinson, Brenda Kuhr, Noel Wilson, Effie Best, Jim Dellitt, Peter Armstrong, Joanne Kemp, Wayne Sawyer, Adam Griffiths, Pamela Ball and Helen Richardson, who reacted to particular chapters.

Finally the book would never have appeared without the continuing encouragement of Ken Watson and the support of my wife, Lynn.

Explanatory Note

There is no single, standard way in which Australian schools label the different year levels of schooling. In this book, the most common system is used. The first year of primary school is year 1. Then follow years 2, 3 and so on up to year 12 which is the final year of secondary school. Secondary school begins in year 8 in South Australia and year 7 in most other states.

General Editor's Introduction

This book is published in the United Kingdom as the secondary schools are preparing and teaching for the new General Certificate of Secondary Education (GCSE). It is already clear that, in all subjects, the assessment procedures for the new examination are going to make different demands upon teachers than those of more traditional patterns of examining. English teachers, many of whom have had a long tradition of internally assessed course work, may take to the new examination more easily than teachers in some other subject areas but, even for them, there remain many questions to be answered about how the new examination system will work. Most important amongst such questions is the likely 'backwash' effect, for good or ill, of the new examination at 16+.

Furthermore, at the same time as we are experimenting with new examining techniques, there is also much discussion of the most appropriate way of reporting the results with a variety of schemes being proposed for student profiling.

Given the range of activities that comprise the English programme in schools and the inherent difficulties in assessing and evaluating such things as response to literature, teachers of English are looking, as much as those of other subjects, for help and advice in this difficult area.

It was against this background of widespread change in the school evaluation policies that I discovered with a sense of excitement the first version present volume when I was working in Australia. It represents a unique achievement. Its author is, as he begins by saying, a professional researcher, and his work has been concerned with exploring ways in which teachers of English can make the assessment of students' work a positive element within their developing skills as users of language and students of literature.

Some of the ideas are by no means new: 'contract learning' goes back at least to the 20s and the days of the Dalton Plan, for example. But, in the light of other current research and developments in practice of process writing (to take one very topical example), it is stimulating and rewarding to have soundly based research evidence for the value of enabling students to reflect upon their own work and to learn from a structured programme of self-evaluation along the lines described here.

The advice which is given in these pages provides a valuable guide to practice for the English teacher in the development of styles of formative evaluation within the classroom. It provides a confirmation and elaboration of the kinds of approaches that have already been pioneered in such as that of Andrew Stibbs in his highly influential pamphlet,

Assessing Children's Language (Ward Lock Education & NATE, 1979). But we are all well aware that what may at times be good classroom practice can often seem to be at odds with the need for public accountability and the purposes fulfilled by the assessment of so key a subject as English in the world beyond the classroom. The particular value of Brian Johnston's book is that it encompasses this challenge to such an extent that its ideas have, in fact, become the basis for the public examination of English in the state of South Australia where the author works as a researcher in the State's Education Department. Chapter 12 of the present volume, in particular, demonstrates how we can lead students to understand and to sympathise with the demands of 'judgemental assesment' without the latter getting in the way of their own developing sense of themselves as successful language users.

In introducing an earlier volume in this series (Robert Protherough's *Teaching Literature for Examinations*, Open University Press, 1986), I quoted Sir Arthur Quiller-Couch writing in 1921: 'We teachers must first learn how to teach. When that is learned, Examination will come as a consequent, easy, almost trivial matter.' The present volume further exemplifies the truth of this remark. Brian Johnston shows convincingly how student-based assessment can be just as rigorous and clear in its objectives as any other form and makes out a sound case for such assessment, based upon the students' setting of their own goals, as a major element within their language learning. Though based upon his research studies the book provides a good deal of help for the practising and hard-pressed classroom teacher. A programme of assessment along the lines proposed here could place examinations in their right place, as the culmination of a schooling-long process of learning how to use language rather than simply as a hurdle to be trained for and jumped over at the end of the course. It is in this hope that I welcome an important new volume to this series and introduce its author to a wider public.

Anthony Adams

1 Assessment and Student Reflection

I am a researcher, not a teacher. For seven years I worked alongside teachers, learning how to help students reflect upon their work in English and humanities classes.

It began with a small research study which eight teachers[1] and I conducted in 1978, under the title, 'Motivational effects of different schemes for assessing students' writing'. The results of the research suggest that when English teachers avoid grades and marks, and involve students in assessing their own work, then the students are more motivated to improve their writing than are students who continuously receive grades or marks.

Reports of the study were published in the proceedings of an educational research conference,[2] in a book on English teaching[3] and in an educational magazine,[4] and included the recommendation that teachers 'encourage student involvement in arriving at assessments by: teaching students self-assessment and peer group assesment skills; teaching students to specify the aspects of their work that they want responses to; and teaching students to negotiate assessments'. But words are cheap. Neither the eight teachers not I knew how we would go about doing those things.

So I have spent much of the last few years finding out how to involve students in the assessment process, in all aspects of English, not just writing. I have observed teachers at work and often tried my own hand. This book is an account of what I have learnt.

In some parts, the book concentrates on what I have been doing in classrooms. Elsewhere, the focus is on teachers who have tried similar things. Most of the work has been done in secondary schools, but the procedures described can be applied in primary and tertiary classes and in subject areas other than English.

In this chapter I discuss how important it is that students reflect on the quality of their work, and I briefly desribe the research study which triggered my interest in this topic.

LEARNING AND REFLECTION

To reflect upon one's own work is part of learning. Kolb, Rubin and McIntyre's[5] 'learning cycle' (Fig. 1) describes how an **active** learner **experiences** things, **reflects** on those experiences, **conceptualizes** what has been learnt and goes on to act on the basis of the conceptualization, that is, **experiments**.

Figure 1: 'The Learning Cycle'

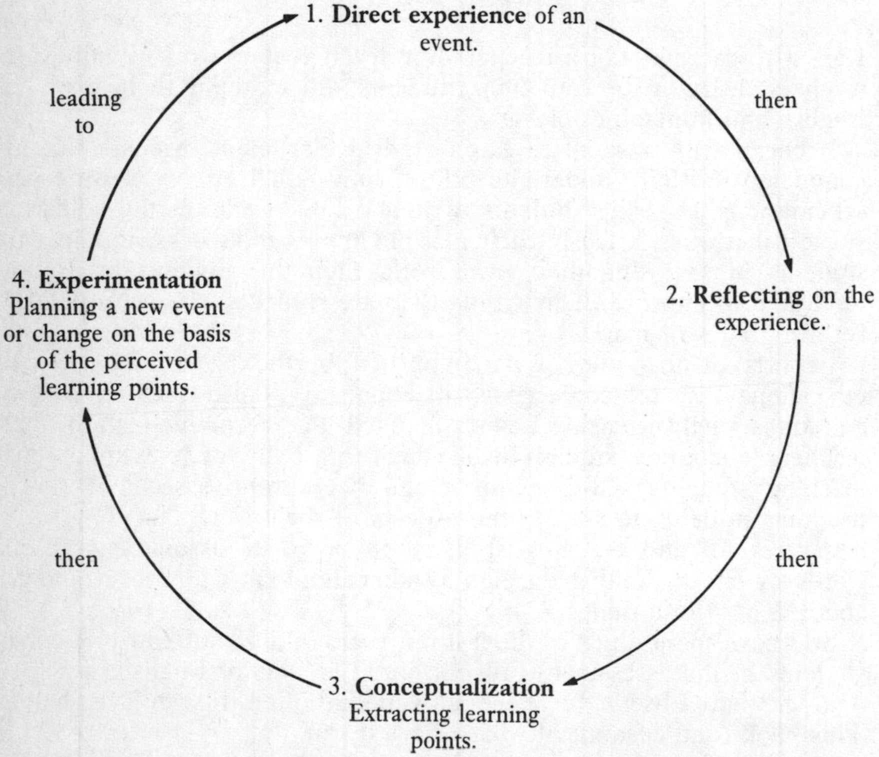

1. **Direct experience** of an
event.

leading
to

then

4. **Experimentation**
Planning a new event
or change on the basis
of the perceived
learning points.

2. **Reflecting** on the
experience.

then

then

3. **Conceptualization**
Extracting learning
points.

Not all activity involves reflection, conceptualization and experimentation. Jimmy Connors is not doing those things every moment he plays tennis, but then often he is not learning tennis, just doing it. So it is with students in English. Simply to be writing does not mean that the student is learning writing.

School students have many experiences of writing, but I suspect that they reflect, conceptualize and experiment only rarely. When asked, 'What did you learn from doing that writing?' or 'What were you experimenting with?', students are often confused. The questions make little sense to them. If they cannot articulate what they are learning, then they are not learning in a way which is conscious and under their control.

If I am right that many students do not reflect, conceptualize and deliberately experiment in English lessons, we should be asking 'Why not?'. Part of the answer is that when teachers are expected to grade or mark each piece of work, then **they** do the reflecting and conceptualizing for the students. In many classes there is a gaping hole in the learning cycle (Fig. 2): students do the work, the teacher assesses it, the students look to see how the assessments compare with what they hoped for, and go straight on to the next experience without even rereading

Figure 2: The teacher interrupts the learning cycle

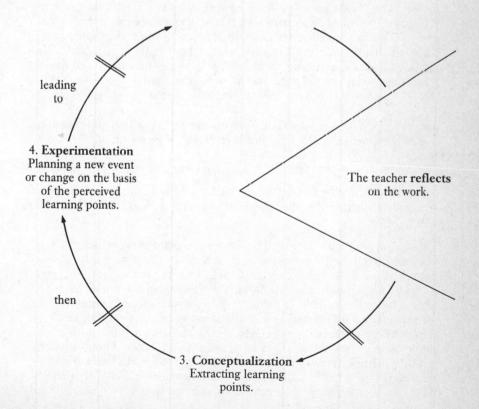

leading
to

4. Experimentation
Planning a new event
or change on the basis
of the perceived
learning points.

The teacher **reflects**
on the work.

then

3. Conceptualization
Extracting learning
points.

their work, let alone reflecting on it. Little wonder that many students make little progress in English in secondary school.

THE INITIAL RESEARCH STUDY

In planning the research, we speculated that teachers' assessments interfere with student learning most seriously when they are recorded as categorical judgements in the form of grades or marks. The formal appearance of a grade or a number encourages all, including the student, to see it as an indicator of a fixed characteristic of the student, rather than as an aspect of the interaction between teacher, the student and the subject matter. To increase the validity of the assessments of this supposed fixed ability, grades or marks from different pieces of work are added up and the average is accepted as a general evaluation of the student. Most significantly, students themselves accept these general assessments as valid, as is illustrated by the following statements from two Western Australian students who were asked to write on 'What Failure in English Means to Me'.[6]

> I think, perhaps, that to fail English is, in a way, to fail as a person of society. The reason for why I have interpreted failing English in this way is because English is concerned with how well you can explain things, the way you talk, how to interpret something, how well you understand, using your initiative, how much insight a person has, to show your ability at reading, writing and talking, to show how creative you can be and many other things that can tell what sort of person you are.
>
> (Year 12 student, government senior high school)

> You ask how it feels to me to fail. Well up till now I've gotten quite used to it. I'm not quite sure why I fail but I do. It sort of grows on one — like a fungus.
>
> (Year 12 student, government senior high school)

Concern at the effects of grading and marking is most commonly felt in relation to students like these who get poor grades. Broadfoot[7] described how:

> The pupil constantly in receipt of negative evaluations which ... the unidimensional value system of the school is likely to apply to his behaviour as well as his academic achievement, learns, for his own protection, to 'play it cool', to devalue these evaluations and develop an alternative value system in which he can experience success. These attempts to defend himself against the sense of failure meted out by the school will be enhanced to the extent that he can band together with other pupils in the same situation. Thus gradually, as teachers know only too well, recalcitrant cliques and infamous classes develop characterized by a rejection of the school's values, and frequently, the elevation of alternative values such as peer group comradeship or machismo.

Teachers usually make herculean efforts to encourage and stimulate these students, but often no amount of understanding or charismatic teaching will succeed. The teacher becomes frustrated and often angry at what appears as a lack of motivation. But the student is far from unmotivated. He is strongly motivated to avoid a sense of being a failure; he is attempting to protect his own sense of self-worth. Paradoxically, he can best avoid a sense of being a failure, someone who is unable to achieve, if he makes little or no effort to achieve. Because then, when he gets a poor grade, he can explain it away by pointing to his lack of effort on a task that he can claim he doesn't value. Whereas, if he had made an effort and still did poorly, that would then be seen by himself and others as demonstrating a lack of ability to achieve.

These failure-avoiding students can also protect themselves when they are forced to set goals, by setting them unrealistically high. The inevitable failure will not then be an indicator of their intrinsic ability.

What of the students who commonly get middling grades like a C? They often use the strategies just described; to get a C by merely coasting along is much better for one's self-esteem, than working very hard and receiving an average grade or mark. These students also suffer from the disadvantage that while the middling grades are the most commonly awarded, they are also the least informative. This was demonstrated in a study conducted in South Australia in 1974.[8] Five classes of Year 10 English students were required to take essays which they had written and which had been graded by the teacher, and predict how the teacher would grade them according to seven separate criteria (grammar, interest level, planning, etc.). The teachers were then required to make separate gradings for each criterion, and the accuracy of the students' predictions was assessed. The students who commonly received As and Us were more than twice as accurate in their predictions as were those who received middling grades.

The crudeness of the traditional grading scheme also means that those students who usually get a C are often unlikely to see any change in their grade, after what might appear to them to be a significant improvement in their work. When these students find that variations in the quality of their work do not seem to affect their grade, the grade comes to be seen as an inevitable result, a function of their acceptable, but unremarkable place in a developing hierarchy. There is little point in making more than a minimal effort to achieve.

And what of the students who usually get 'good' grades? Grading is often justified on the grounds that it motivates students, and research[9] gives some support to this claim for that proportion of students who generally receive high grades. While some of these students are oriented to work effectively towards success and to accept the occasional lower grade as a stimulus to further endeavour, others, who are labelled successful, are motivated primarily by fear of failure. Covington and Beery describe them as **overstrivers**, characterized by high ability, overpreparedness and excessive attention to detail. They have grown up with a sense that one's achievements define one's worth. Consequently, they work compulsivley to avoid failure, and because of the amount of effort they expend, they are all the more easily threatened; for if they were to fail they could not attribute it to lack of effort. Consequently, these students regard failure at school with a dread that is far out of proportion to its actual significance. 'Like all failure-avoiding students, the overstriver has fallen victim to a misunderstanding of the proper role of failure in the learning process'.[10]

There is another cause for concern at the effect grading has on students, both successful and unsuccessful. By providing clear and powerful rewards for writing that are quite separate from the writing itself, students are distracted from appreciating the intrinsic satisfaction of writing. A body of research is accumulating[11] to show that when a task can be enjoyable, and best performance is not achieved by following mechanical rules, then providing rewards for completing the task has detrimental effects on the learner's motivation to continue with that type of activity when the rewards are no longer offered. When the emphasis is on being rewarded for doing the task the learner's attention becomes geared to mechanical procedures and their enjoyment of it wanes: it becomes an onerous chore.

This incompatibility between an emphasis on external rewards and the development of intrinsic motivation was discussed by Marx in 1844. The relevance of his concept of the worker being alienated when his labour is reduced to commodity value, is made clear in the following passage, where 'writing' has been substituted for 'work' and 'student' for 'worker'.

> His (writing) is not voluntary but imposed, forced labour. It is not the satisfaction of a need but only the means of satisfying other needs. Its alien character is clearly shown by the fact that as soon as there is no physical or other compulsion it is avoided like the plague. Finally the alienated character of (writing) for the (student) appears in the fact that it is not his (writing) but (writing) for someone else....[12]

Our concern was to develop assessment approaches which might avoid these problems. At first it was not easy to define alternative methods. At times we were almost ready to agree with Hextall's complaint. '*The pain and mystery of this for me is that such a fundamentally quantitative, calculative orientation to work is so embedded that an alternative version is literally inconceivable.*'[13] Slowly we developed a theory which described characteristics of assessment schemes which might be more effective motivationally than the traditional, judgemental approach of grading or marking. To test a theory was important because we wanted to be confident that when we came to collect data from schools, we would be able to draw conclusions from it, and do more than simply report back. The theory can be conveniently described in terms of five guidelines for teachers, which the teachers and I considered to be valuable suggestions for developing a **responsive**, as compared to **judgemental** assessment scheme. Because the research study focused only on writing, we now move from a general discussion of the relationship between assessment and learning to the particular example of assessment of writing. Nevertheless, the guidelines presented can be applied to assessment more generally, both in English and other subjects, and this is demonstrated in the later chapters of this book.

Five proposed guidelines for a responsive assessment scheme

1. **Don't record a judgement of the worth of every piece of writing.** While it is difficult to imagine a situation where teachers **never** gave an overall evaluation of the worth of a piece of work, it obviously need not happen with every piece of writing. If students are to be encouraged to write often, they should be able to write without there being a continual threat of evaluation. Deferring evaluation is a powerful stimulus to production of ideas[14] and high-quality student writing comes from students whose focal concentration is on the ideas they are trying to express.[15] Many professional writers' accounts attest to the value of encouraging production while deferring evaluation. Virginia Woolf provides an example.[16]

   > Still if it were not written rather faster than the fastest type-writing, if I stopped and took thought, it would never be written at all; and the advantage of the method is that it sweeps up accidentally several stray matters which I should exclude if I hesitated, but which are the diamonds of the dust-heap.

2. **Avoid recording reactions to a piece in terms of a formal record, like a grade or number.** These give a seeming objectivity to what is often, with writing, a largely subjective response by the teacher. The subjectivity does not render the reaction less accurate, impartial or fair. But because the reaction has a subjective component it therefore needs to be described all the more carefully, if it is to be clearly understood by the student. Another problem with seemingly formal records is that they imply to many people that a relatively fixed characteristic is being assessed, and they can be the basis for self-fulfilling prophesies which can limit students' development.

3. **Be specific in describing the aspects of a piece of writing which are being responded to.** Clearly it is difficult for a student to improve his writing if he is unaware of particular aspects of his writing that he might change. At any one time, teacher and student should share an understanding of at least one specific aspect of

writing that the particular student is to consider working on. Without this, exhortations to improve would seem doomed to failure.

Furthermore, if the student knows which aspects of his writing are being responded to, he is less lilely to take the reaction as a reflection of his general worth.

4. **Encourage student involvement in arriving at assessments by:** teaching students self-assessment skills; teaching students peer-group assessment skills; teaching students to specify the aspects of their work that they want responded to; and teaching students to negotiate assessments.

    Giving students practice at assesing pieces of writing is a valuable part of providing information and models to help them write well; and after all, when the students leave school there will not be a teacher to do the assessing. Furthermore, student involvement in the process also makes clearer the joint responsibility that teacher and student share both for the quality of the learning and for the written products. Encouraging students to behave responsibly in this way is also a powerful means of expressing to them that their views about their own work are important.

    Finally, the ability to make accurate assessments of ourselves, our products and our future goals is a basic characteristic of a psychologically healthy person. Teachers have a responsibility to foster students' ability to make accurate self-assessments, if for no reason other than to balance out the alienating effects of the labelling they are forced to do at report writing time.

5. **Encourage students to revise work after it has been commented upon.** When this approach is used, a piece of writing is being treated as something that develops, rather than as a static entity. We suggest that students will be less likely to see grades (for example) as labelling fixed characteristics of them, if they see how, through redrafting, writing can become a co-operative exercise. This approach makes it clear that a grade is a description of an interaction between teacher and student, and not a comment on the student in isolation.

SURVEY OF ENGLISH TEACHERS

We then set up a research study to test the thcory that assessment schemes which follow the five guidelines are associated with students being more encouraged to improve their writing.

The first question we had to address was whether we could develop a reliable method of measuring teachers' assessment schemes that covered those elements seen to be important in our theory.

We investigated this by surveying the English teachers in every secondary school (state and private) in South Australia. One thousand and six teachers completed a structured questionnaire which required them to describe the degree to which their assessing followed our five guidelines. Analysis of the teachers' responses showed that a single reliable scale for measuring assessment schemes could be taken from the questionnaire, if the specificity of the teacher's assessment (the third guideline) was ignored. Teacher specificity was not positively correlated with the other aspects of a responsive scheme and it was not considered in the main study.

FOLLOW-UP OF SURVEY

Our next task was to approach a smaller number of teachers whose assessment practices covered the range from judgemental to responsive, and to collect data from their students concerning their motivation to improve their writing. The individual teachers' questionnaires identified the school they came from, but not the particular teacher concerned. We approached a sample of schools whose questionnaires reported a range of varied assesment practices, explained our reasons for selecting that school, and asked for two volunteer teachers of Year 10 English who exemplified the practice that we had identified from that school's questionnaires. We collected data from 36 teachers; again both state and private schools were involved, both metropolitan and country.

In order to check that we had accurate knowledge of these teachers' assessment practices we got them to complete the questionnaire again, while explaining to us the reasons for their responses. A further check was made when we gave the students taught by these teachers a questionnaire to gauge their response to the assessment scheme they operated under. Some questions concerned the degree to which students were involved in the assessment process, and in the 34 classes finally included, the students provided a strong confirmation of the descriptions provided by the teachers. (In two classes, the students' responses threw the validity of the teacher's report into question. After further discussion with the teachers it was clear that they had misled us and those classes were omitted from the analysis.)

We were then ready to investigate the question of central concern: do students who work under a responsive assessment scheme report being motivated to improve their written work as a result of the assessment more often than students working under a judgemental scheme? In our questionnaire to students we included items which were indicators of the students' motivation to improve after assessment. They covered such questions as 'Do you practice improving your work by doing some parts of an assignment again after it has been assessed?', 'Do you try to improve your work the next time, in the way the teacher has indicated?',

'If the teacher spends a lot of time writing comments about your work, does this encourage you to work harder?', and 'Do you feel like giving up because you get the same assessment time after time?' and formed a reliable nine-item scale.

MAIN FINDINGS

The students' motivation scores were averaged for each class, and the class average was then correlated with the score indicating the responsiveness of the teacher's assessment scheme. The Pearson correlation obtained was .52 ($df = 32$, $p < .01$) giving strong support to our theory that a responsive scheme is more effective motivationally than a judgemental scheme.

We were aware that this finding might have been caused by other factors. For example, the teachers who used a responsive assessment scheme might have been more popular with their students and this may explain why their students reported being motivated more by assessments. We examined this possibility after getting the classes involved to indicate how much they liked their teacher, and found that there was no significant difference in popularity between the responsive and the judgemental teachers. Therefore the students' liking for the teacher played no role in causing our main finding. In addition, further analysis suggested that it did not come about because of different levels of achievement (as assessed by teachers' gradings) of the different classes.

While the more responsive approaches to assessment seemed clearly superior, in terms of their motivational effects, when the average scores for each class were considered, it was of interest to ponder whether this superiority applied when only the students who were getting A grades were considered, for these successful students are rewarded under the judgemental scheme. Perhaps a judgemental scheme might be most appropriate for these successful students, and a responsive scheme more suitable for other students. An analysis involving only A students was possible because all but three of the teachers were required to provide ratings for the school assessment periods. This showed that the A students' motivation scores were marginally higher under the more responsive approaches, but this was not a significant effect. *It seems therefore that when there is less emphasis on a judgemental approach to assessment, A students do not suffer a disadvantage and the less successful students are more motivated to improve.*

Appendix 1 reports some secondary findings of this study, relating the type of assessment scheme to students' competitiveness, the students' perception of being treated fairly or unfairly and the reasons they thought teachers had for assessing them. (A more technical report of the research is B. Johnston, 'Responding to students writing' in M. J. Lawson and R. Linke, eds *Inquiry and Action in Education*. Adelaide: Australian Association for Research in Education, 1981.)

CONCLUSION

This study was satisfying in that it provided a coherent picture of some educational implications of different approaches to assessment. However, it was of limited use to teachers. When I conducted in-service training sessions to explore the research and its implications, most teachers said that they needed to be shown ways of following the five guidelines, and in particular ways of involving students in self-assessment, peer assessment and negotiating assessments. I found I needed to go back to some of the schools in the study, and to others, to get a more detailed and systematic account of how teachers did these things. The teachers' strategies are presented in Chapters Three to Twelve. In Chapter Two, I discuss how attempts to involve students in the assessment process often fail because of the climate created by the school's assessment practices.

2 Do Schools' Assessment Structures Encourage Students to Reflect on Their Learning?

To create an environment in which students seriously reflect on their work, a school needs an assessment structure which

- is principally to aid students' development, rather than a means of controlling them through rewards and punishments.

- allows students to experiment safely. If the students' reflections do not lead them to try new things, as described in the learning cycle (p. 2), they will soon see little point in the reflection process.

- encourages students to dwell on the specifics of their experiences of learning, rather than mimic the judgemental language of traditional school assessments.

The subsequent chapters provide strategies for achieving these three things. This chapter describes how most schools, even those which are developing new approaches to assessment, fail to achieve these conditions and consequently interfere with the classroom teacher's attempts to involve students in meaningful assessment of their own learning.

AIDING STUDENTS' DEVELOPMENT

School policy statements and syllabuses often assert that the primary purpose of assessment is to promote student development. Nevertheless schools' assessment practices ususaly contradict these philosophical statements. Assessments of student attitude provide a very clear example.

Students' report cards often carry an attitude grading, which may be from the range, '+ +, +, 0, −, − −'; or an interest category where the teacher ticks either 'interested' or 'shows little interest'. The purpose of these assessments is not to aid students' development. They do not need to be told what their attitude is. These assessments are crude attempts at social control: compliant students are rewarded with '+ +' and students who are disruptive or bored are punished with '− −', which is an act of retaliation, not education.

Black and Broadfoot have claimed that assessments of attitude, interest and effort have 'potential for diagnosing problems which pupils are having with the development of now-cognitive characteristics, and consequently, offering potential for the reinforcement of such qualities. It may well be that where an aspect such as motivation is explicitly recognized through assessment as a key factor in learning, this can provide a channel of communication through which motivation can actually be improved.'[1] They go on to present examples of such assessment, including this five-point scale for standardized reporting of students' attitudes:

1. Keen and interested
   Works hard at all times

2. Works very steadily
   Shows some interest and enthusiasm

3. Works erratically
   Works well when interested

4. Easily satisfied with an inferior job
   Requires constant prodding

5. Apathetic
   Lazy and uninterested.

To see students' motivation or attitude as a characteristic to be developed along such a continuum is frighteningly mechanistic, especially if it is seen as basically the students' responsibility to 'brush up their attitude'. And this is how it it usually understood by the time attitude gradings like these are on report cards. Categories 4 and 5 are insults hardly worthy of the title 'non-cognitive assessments'. Where is the category for the student who gave the course a fair go, but eventually decided it was not for her? Or for the student who does competent work on set tasks, but is mostly interested in life outside the classroom? And what of a student who shows a discriminating response to (say) a number of set texts by working hard on some and giving only a token effort on others? Does that intelligent response really need to be diagnosed and 'developed' into 'works very steadily', with the final graduation to 'works hard at all times'?

Black and Broadfoot are right when they suggest that assessments of students' motivation are an important part of teaching. They are the subject of the next chapter of this book. But these assessments should recognize that motivation is a product of the students' interaction with the setting and the tasks. They are not the proper focus of an educational report on a student which may go to parents, prospective employers and higher education authorities. Students should be free to work sometimes faster, sometimes slower; and to express negative reactions to texts and tasks, without fear of being handicapped by negative or middling reports on their attitude. In fact one of the teacher's most difficult tasks is to legitimize expression of rebellious energies, so that classes do not remain an unhappy mixture of dependent and rebellious students, but instead assertively choose to channel their energies to the parts of the curriculum they most value.

ALLOWING STUDENTS TO EXPERIMENT SAFELY

Experimenting and reflection are fundamental to learning which empowers the student. Donald Graves has demonstrated that when students experiment with new forms in writing, the quality of their work is very inconsistent. Often established skills break down while the student concentrates on the yet-to-be-mastered experiment.

When assessments are based mainly on examinations, students have some leeway to experiment at other times. However the current emphasis on assessment by the classroom teacher continuously throughout the year makes such experimentation a risky business indeed.

Many students feel that they are liable to be judged every time they open their mounths in class and every time they write for the teacher. And they are right to think this way in systems where their teachers draw on informal personal contacts to complete 'pupil profiles'[2] in which they rate students' listening, speaking, and so on.

Imagine you are teaching a class of thirty students, twenty-five of whom appear to listen attentively to almost all discussions and presentations. Three seem to attend about half the time and two only listened attentively on two occasions that you remember, when their friends gave talks on drugs and fixing motor cycles. Would you give all the students the same rating on listening, because they had all demonstrated competence? Most teachers would not. They would give the last two students a lower rating, as if infrequent listening indicated a lack of competence! And they would justify it as an attempt to be **fair** to the other students.

Students show two contrasting reactions in this all-too-common situation. Inevitably, some begin to play safe. They ask questions and offer opinions only when they think that these will be judged to be sensible. They do not voice their difficulties. They avoid experimenting for fear of making errors. Yet it is often the apparently silly question that reveals where students most need help and it is often only through risk-taking — in speech or writing — that we expand our linguistic range.

Many other students give up. They cannot imagine themselves consistently doing well, so 'why bother at all?'. Rather than being set clearly defined goals which they could make a special effort to achieve, they are expected to make the effort all the time. They will not. Their restless spirits are stronger than that.

When the actual behaviour assessed is more clearly specified than in pupil profiles, for example assessment of essays on a regular basis throughout the year, it is quite common under continuous assessment for students who want to do well to have to do so **consistently throughout the year**. This is more a continual trial than a learning situation. The shameful thing about the common practice of mindlessly averaging grades or marks over a whole year is that students who need teaching early in the year (for example, a year 11 student who in the first term retells the story of a text rather than discussing it), are saddled with poor marks which progressively limit the degree to which they can score well at the end of the year, even if they were to achieve a high standard by then. So continuous assessment can act as a powerful disincentive to learning and teaching. Some teachers tell me that they would ignore early marks if they saw a dramatic improvement by the end of the year. But if students are not aware that this is how the final grades are to be arrived at, then they will see little point in an improvement late in the year.

AVOIDING MIMICKING THE LANGUAGE OF TRADITIONAL SCHOOL ASSESSMENTS

Systems which rely on continuous assessment and include grades for attitude put the purpose of judgement and social control above that of enhancing student development. Students are very familiar with assessment as a control mechanism and their experience of it affects how they think about themselves as learners. The most central issue is not positive or negative self-esteem, but whether students' self-concepts as learners are based firmly in their own experience — or are mediated by and dependent on teachers' concepts of them.

If we want to assess ways in which to encourage students to reflect on their own work, we must be careful that we are not in such a hurry that we try to squeeze assessments out of them before they have reflected on the **specifics** of their experience. If we do that they will simply mimic the language that presently dominates assessment in schools, the language of judgement. In so doing, they will use other people's labels: what they write and say will not be grounded in their own experience.

This section presents some examples of students reflecting in a language which is not their own. The examples are presented because they are commonly described as self-assessment and they are the opposite of what this book is working towards.

School report cards sometimes have a small space for students' self-assessment and comments like these often appear:

'I am good at English'
'I am not good at English'
'I am good at writing essays'.

Students who write comments like these are making global judgements of themselves, just as teachers do if they talk about good and bad students.

These self-assessments do not help students develop. On the contrary, if they have any effect on them at all, it is to reinforce them labelling themselves in ways which limit their self-perceptions. Each of the above examples, although more specific than 'I am clever' or 'I am stupid', are too general to be true, let alone useful; for no-one is always bad at every task that English involves, and no-one does well on every aspect of essay writing each time they write. If I have a problem in English it applies in a specific context, and I'll not handle that problem till I stop labelling myself and work towards specifying when I experience that problem and what I might do about it.

Facing the specific problems can be hard work and students often avoid that challenge by deciding that they are either good or bad in certain areas of the curriculum. They either have 'got it' or they haven't.

Now when **we** encourage them to think in terms of being generally good or bad at something, we are actually encouraging them to **avoid** learning. Of course this is precisely the opposite of educating, but, unfortunately, it is very common in schools and actively promoted by those who encourage teachers to differentiate so-called 'above-average', 'average' and 'below average' students.

More descriptive approaches to assessment do not necessarily avoid these problems. For example, Colin Fletcher[3] provides the following self-assessment from a pupil profile and Black and Broadfoot[4] considered it worth quoting in their book as an example of student involvement in assessment.

TEACHER'S COMMENTS

J. must learn to discipline herself to work according to the pattern established. She had a very slow start but has improved later and is now making some progress. She does not find the subject easy and will have to work really hard at it.

Signed: E. Smith   Dated: 12.12.1981

J., within the limits of her ability, has continued to make progress. She seems to be enjoying the work and recently has done really well.

Signed: E. Smith   Dated: 9.6. 1982

PUPIL'S COMMENTS

I will try to discipline myself and work harder in maths. I think it is a fair comment.

Signed: Joanne Jones   Dated: 15.12.1981

I am pleased with this comment and I think I do enjoy the work we do.

Signed: Joanne Jones   Dated: 9.6.1982

PARENT'S COMMENTS

Pleased J is making some progress in this subject. I think she has always found the subject hard.

Signed: P.G. Jones

Is Joanne's parrotting of the teacher's inarticulate definition of her work supposed to help her — or anyone else? She **thinks** she enjoys the work. It seems she is uncertain about how she feels, but if the teacher thinks she is enjoying it, well she will think that too! She and her parents are **pleased** that she is making progress within the unknowable 'limits of her ability'!

It is odd that this is put forward as a positive model. Fletcher tells us that it is part of 'a grounded alternative': 'less human modes of assessment would be the seeds of alienation'. But the language of that example is itself a seed of alienation. Both student and parent express satisfaction with, and adopt, a language which is too ungrounded to help them. They have been distracted from noticing that there is no indication at all of what Joanne can or cannot actually do in the subject.

Here is a much more detailed student self-assessment from a year 7 boy: it also illustrates how the language of judgemental assessment can act as a barrier, or at the very least, a distraction, to a truthful record of a student's activity.

Self-Evaluation

I enjoy reading and usually read mysteries. I mainly read in my spare time. When using a dictionary, I usually feel confident. In group work I don't work very well because I can't concentrate properly, I'm not comfortable when I talk to the class because I am very restless. I enjoy Sport, Art, and Music but don't enjoy Drama very much. I don't listen well when others are speaking. I don't communicate to other people very well because I usually don't know what I'm saying.

I like the idea of sharing writing with other people and I'm very happy about it. I need to polish up my writing much better than usual because I'm not satisfied with my work.

No, I haven't presented my work neatly and I need a lot of help in my spelling.

George

George's teacher had talked to the children about what they did in class and during the discussion she blackboarded some questions which they used as a guide when they wrote. The self-assessments were typed onto a report card and sent home to parents at the end of term.

To the extent that George believes what he has written, he is not only saddled with a very negative self-concept ('I don't work very well', 'I can't concentrate properly', 'I'm not comfortable when I talk to the class', 'I don't listen well', 'I don't communicate to other people very well', 'I usually don't know what I'm saying', 'I'm not satisfied with my work'), but worse, he believes in a lie, a delusion about himself, for no-one is chronically incapable of knowning his own meanings ('I don't know what I'm saying'). This is tantamount to George denying the validity of his reactions in the classroom. Nor is any person continually or categorically poor at listening to others ('I don't listen well') or incapable of concentrating ('I can't concentrate properly').

As it stands George's self-assessment leaves him powerless and dependent, a bundle of needs and problems. There are no clear guides to action in the self-assessment. The weaknesses are described as if they apply generally rather than in specific definable situations and they are located squarely within his self. Improvement can only come if one part of the self battles to overcome another part, a divisive tension which is as likely to succeed as lifting oneself up by one's boot straps. How likely is it that George will overcome such a range of weaknesses? And what justification is there for self-assessment if it doesn't lead to productive action?

Of course self-assessments are not always as negative as George's. Some are positive judgements about strengths. Even so, in as much as they refer to strengths as if they are fixed characteristics of the person, rather than specific achievements in a particular context, they act to define limits on the student, feeding a concept of self which is vulnerable to changing situations.

Anna, a year 8 student, provided an example of this when talking to me recently about her writing, which her teacher described as drab and ordinary.

Brian: Do you think that he (the teacher) will be interested in your piece of writing?

Anna: Yeah.

Brian: How come? What is in it that will interest him?

Anna: I don't know. He's interested in everything.

(later)

Brian: I reckon it would be a better piece of writing if you put some detail in it about how you actually know that she was enjoying herself more. Do you reckon it would be a better piece doing that?

Anna: It doesn't really make any difference to me. Usually Mr. T. writes comments on my writing. I just look at them and they don't have any effect on me.

Brian: Is that because you're not interested in becoming a better writer?

Anna: Well, when I was in year 6 we had to do compositions and the teacher always used to write on my paper, 'Good, well done!' and 'Good, well written!'. So I don't see any reason why my writing needs to improve.

Anna read 'Good, well done!' to mean that she was good at English and became so concerned about being a superior student that she was distracted from learning.

The vulnerability of students like Anna often becomes apparent when they enter the senior secondary years where English is dominated by the demands of literary study. In junior secondary, they have been rewarded with high grades for trying hard, complying and writing neatly and correctly. In year 11 they find that they are no longer 'good at English'. Some of these people have staked a lot on English being something they are good at and they feel devastated by a C grade. They then get furious with the English teacher. They think she is victimizing them — and the teacher certainly is a threat to their very fragile self-concepts.

Here are two students who, right in the middle of this experience, are writing in their learning records:

Judy: Last year I was told I had the ability to write a good essay and the beginning of this year I felt really confident, but now I feel I'm not sure. I hate it. You are destroying our ideas, taking our identities and English ideas away from us.

Christine: He could have given me a 'B' at least. I understood what I wrote and knew what I was getting at. He obviously didn't read between the lines. I feel I can understand almost anything I read so I don't need to help myself in that area.

These students had reputations as good students (Christine had never before got below an A), yet they were ignorant of what specifically they had done to get their A's. Instead of giving them articulate feedback, their teachers had told them they did good work. This left them dependent on teachers to continue to support a self-concept whose fragility came from the generalized, inarticulate feedback they had been getting.

Donald Graves describes students like these two, who are dependent on teachers' concepts of them as good students.

You know the toughest person to work with,
the straight A student
who somewhere around the age of nine became
an intellectual prostitute.
They learned to play the game and got so good at it,
that they could figure out which way the wind was blowing ...
but at every point they were denying their
own voices.
They sold out, sold out, sold out,
and when it came time now that a professor said
'Your voice is weak. Put yourself in there' ...
they couldn't do it.
These were students who were despising their education
even though they were top students.[5]

By the time students are in the middle years of secondary schooling, categorical thinking about themselves in relation to school, the big evaluative institution in their lives, is quite firmly set. This was demonstrated when Geraldine McOmish and I got year 10 students at Mt. Barker High School to write a dialogue between their self and their writing. In these three extracts, which were typical, the students projected a very judgemental voice into their writing — and it had the last say!

Writing:	If you had studied more, you may've done better.
Self:	I have other things to do you know! I can never think of things to write.
Writing:	Some people have it and some people don't.

Writing:	I was very surprised that you read through your notes and crossed out what you didn't need. I was very surprised. but it is a pity that you can't keep up the standard.

Writing:	Try writing it down first in small words, then change them into big words and adjectives.
Self:	Why didn't I think of that?
Writing:	We can't all have the brains in this world.

These students are alienated from their own resourcefulness as writers. To take the third student as an example, his strongest voice describes him as being too stupid to think of changing his wording: yet he clearly can think of doing that, because he made the suggestion, while in the role of the writing.

If we want students' reflection to lead to learning, we will help them to avoid global labels and instead use language which specifically describes what they are doing in particular contexts. This book presents many ways of encouraging that type of reflection.

THE PRIMARY PURPOSE OF ASSESSMENT: SOCIAL CONTROL OR EDUCATION?

Despite their anti-educational role, assessment schemes which emphasize continuous labelling of students are maintained by nervous administrators, teachers who can not safely allow their students to work inconsistently and by parents and students who hope to be rewarded for their compliance in following the rules. These groups believe that 'it is **fairer** to have all class work taken into account for assessment'.[6]

Measurement specialists add the notion of reliability of assessments to the debate. They say that assessments should be generalizable. Their basic questions are: 'How do you usually perform in English? How are you likely to perform in the future? What are the limits of your abilities in English?'

But the teacher who chooses to emphasize the role of helping students rather than judging them has a very different attitude to assessment: 'How well can you do this particular task? Let's stretch that a bit. Let's see if with my help you can excel yourself. Let's aim for something that's so good that maybe it would be difficult to repeat it. Let's focus on your best performance.'

So this teacher feels an obligation to aim for assessments which will often be quite **unreliable**, because they focus on what the student is just learning to do. This book is about teachers who have that attitude to assessment; who give a higher priority to helping students than to judging them. In chapters Three to Nine, I describe how teachers can **monitor** students' work in class so as to help them describe what they can do and what they might experiment with and learn next. These monitoring procedures work best when the students know that their experiments and mistakes will be treated as confidential to the learning process: that only their successes need be carried into the judgement situation.

Chapters Ten to Thirteen describe how judgements of the equality of students' work can be organized so that students approach judgement with a view to carefully and knowingly putting their best foot forward in a performance for judges from outside the classroom.

3 Monitoring the Students' Relationship to the Subject Matter

Measurement specialists often suggest that the first assessment task should be some form of **pre-testing**. For example, a teacher could collect a sample of the students' writing across a range of genres and contexts and from that assess what the students can do in writing and what they might be ready to learn.

I have heard this possibility talked about often enough, but I have never known a teacher who did it. One problem would be that if a lot of writing was required early and quickly, the teacher would probably alienate many students who would find themselves writing for a very limited purpose, so that the teacher could see what they were capable of. Writers usually concentrate better and work harder when they care about getting their message across to a reader who will respond to **what** they are writing, not **how** they are writing. Consequently the pre-testing approach runs the danger of not representing what students are capable of when they see more purpose in writing.

Nevertheless, English teachers often do begin a topic or unit of work by assessing; the primary focus is not 'How advanced are the students along certain dimensions of growth in English?', but rather, 'What is their relationship to the subject matter to be addressed?'. So the assessment is qualitative not quantitative. And this assessment is made both when the subject matter is tightly specified (e.g. a particular text) and when students are offered a wider range of choices (e.g. writing personal anecdotes).

Teaching English often involves asking the students 'Where do you stand in relation to this?'. When this is the focus at the beginning of a series of lessons, the students reflect on what they bring to the subject matter, their starting points. With that as a basis they can go on to make connections between what they already know and what they will discover or make more explicit.

By carefully nurturing this reflective process, teachers create a classroom environment which encourages useful student reflection on learning. This contrasts with simply imposing tasks and only asking the students to reflect on them after they are finished. When that happens, students usually see that their reflections do not affect what happens in the classroom and they see little point in them.

This chapter presents four examples of how teachers can begin a series of lessons by involving students in assessing where they stand in relation to the subject matter. As soon as the students begin to articulate their positions, the task of English has begun. The teacher's role is then to encourage the students to explore and deepen their responses. That is a subtle, ongoing process which simultaneously involves teaching and monitoring students' development.

The first three examples are presented initially without comment.

THREE EXAMPLES

First example: year 12 students and Donne's love poetry

Lola Brown was to teach the love poetry of John Donne to a year 12 class at Elizabeth High School. Before the class read any of the poems, Lola and the students together mapped out some of what they already knew about love. They made this word tree.

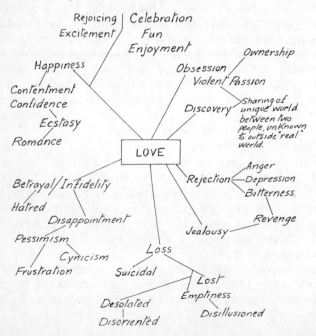

From her knowledge of the poetry, Lola had introduced 'celebration', 'betrayal' and 'infidelity', each of which stimulated reflection by the students.

In forming this map, the students were asserting their connections with love and with all those who have experienced love. They could see some of the ground they were to cover in their study and that it was based on experiences like their own: that they could legitimately say 'I can relate to this poetry and evaluate how it matches my experience'.

Second example: year 8 and year 11 students and personal anecdotes from childhood

Joy Allen of Eudunda Area School wanted year 8 and year 11 classes to write personal recollections from their childhood.

> I walked in with a teddy bear and some little cars, and we just sat around. I had a teddy bear when I was a kid and I talked about how it really mattered to me. And the kids just spontaneously talked about memories from their childhood. Some kids said 'Look, teddy bears don't turn me on. I don't have anything to say about teddy bears' and I said. 'O.K., what about cars'. And we vroom, vroomed around the room for a while. Some of the kids didn't have anything that was triggered by that so I asked them to bring something in that had really mattered to them, or if they couldn't, did they have a photograph of something? So, in the end, each had talked and had a visual representation of what they were going to write about.'

Third example: year 10 students set the task to 'explore an issue in writing'

Joy Allen wanted her year 10 class to explore an issue in writing an expository piece.

> I wrote 'reflect' on the board. We talked about what the heck it means to reflect anyway. That's really hard. Questions which say 'react and reflect upon ...' are really hard for the kids to come to grips with.
>
> Then I did a visualization exercise. I've been using that quite a bit lately. I had them sit down, 'relax, get quiet, muscles aren't there anymore, heads clear'. And they buy that. Their reactions to that are very good. I had everybody visualize a ball, and we talked about the ball. They described it: what size?, what shape?, what colour? — everything about the ball from the outside. How does it feel? Then I said 'O.K. now, go inside the ball... What is inside the ball?'
>
> It was different, of course, for different kids. For some it was space, for some foam, for some rubber. And they really delved into what it was like inside. What does it feel like inside there? Can you come up with things that it is really like?
>
> And after we'd talked, I said 'O.K., that is what reflection is like.'
>
> Visualizing the ball and going inside it was a metaphor for what reflection is. And that seemed to work well.

A really important thing is to get the kids quiet and relaxed. I'm so confident visualizing works. I don't think I've ever had enough resistance to have to say, 'Well will you go along with me on this?' or 'Will you just watch while the others do it, listen to what they say when they've done it and then see if you'll be willing to try it?'

So I said 'That's what reflection is like. Now choose something that really matters to you. If you choose something that you aren't really interested in thinking about any more, going inside it and seeing how it feels and tastes and smells, what it's like in there, it won't be for you. So you've got to find something you really care about.'

And we covered a blackboard that runs the length of the room with things like: 'Death. What is life? Black holes. What are words'?' All the important questions. I was just blown away with the powerful stuff the kids came up with.

And the writing! The intent with which those kids then wrote was fantastic. And for most of them it was the best writing I've had from them.'

Discussion of the first three examples

There are parallels between what Lola and Joy did, and Betty Jean Wagner's[1] account of how Dorothy Heathcote assesses students' relationships to the subject matter in her work using drama in education. By drawing out similarities between these teachers we can identify some of the elements of this subtle assessment process.

The three teachers **start with a very specific stimulus**. In Joy's examples there is the teddy bear, the blackboarded word 'reflect' and the imaginary ball. Lola has the blackboarded word 'love'. 'Sometimes Heathcote begins a drama with concrete objects — a wedding ring, an old musket, a rare coin ... a letter yellowed with age, a skull — to arrest the attention of the group and help their belief.'[2]

Joy (in the second example) and Heathcote then **express their personal relationship to the specific stimulus and wait for students to express their relationships to it**. In Joy's case her personal anecdote encouraged the students to share theirs — or to distance themsleves from the particular instance — 'Teddy bears don't turn me on'.

The goal is that the **students, through articulating their relationship to a specific stimulus, sense and express a connection with a more general human experience**, which Heathcote calls a **universal**. 'Drama, like all art, starts with a very carefully selected, precise and particular, unrepeatable instance — one that then acquires significance as it reverberates in the chambers of the universal.'[3]

So while they observe and listen, these teachers are assessing whether the students have specific experiences or concerns which they can draw on in considering more general aspects of the human condition. Lola **watches** to see if her students can relate their own knowledge and experiences to poetry of love and betrayal. Joy **listens** to hear if her students can identify a treasured object which would trigger recollections from childhood. In the third example, Joy **records** on the blackboard specific concerns which indicate that her students are reflecting on unresolved mysteries of life.

In this context, part of the significance of the individual student's reflection — be it on love, a childhood toy or an unanswered question of life — is that when they express the reflection they assert a connection and commonality with their classmates and the teacher.

Finally both Joy and Heathcote **respond to students who are reluctant to engage in the task by recognizing and respecting their resistance**. So the teacher's focus is on the student's present relationship to the subject matter, not on what it 'should' be. Joy would say 'Will you go along with me on this?' or 'Will you just watch …?' When engagement is low, Heathcote confronts the students with that: 'Hold it a minute. I don't believe you care about this, so unless you can prove you care, I'm going to stop it. I can believe in (it) … Can you?'[4]

FOURTH EXAMPLE: NEGOTIATING THE CURRICULUM

Of course students know only too well that not all the knowledge which is relevant to the English curriculum is within them. Their commitment to learning new external knowledge can be heightened by having them indicate what they know and what they want to know about a particular topic. Processes for doing this are documented in *Negotiating the Curiculum*, edited by Garth Boomer. In that book, Jon Cook outlines four questions which students can address:

1) What do we know already? (that we don't need to learn or be taught about).

2) What do we want to find out? (What are our questions, problems, curiosities and challenges?)

3) How will we go about finding out? (Where will we look? What will we read? Who will do what?, and what should be the order of things?)

4) How will we know, and show that we've got there? (What are our findings? What have we learnt? Whom will we show? For whom are we doing the work?)[5]

So in this approach, the students assess their relationship to the topic in a very deliberate, explicit way.

As in the first three examples, an important role for the teacher is to assess the students' answers to see that they are, on the one hand, **specific** topics or explorations, and on the other, **that they relate to the concerns of the class as a whole**. So when students suggest work, the teacher and other students should reflect upon it and develop a sense of how it relates to the overall class work. The teacher asks such questions as 'What would be the point of that?', 'Where would it lead us?' and 'Tell us more about why we need to know that.' If this sense of connection with overall class work is lacking, reports to the class are seen as boring. The other students have little sense of how the reports relate to what they have been doing and the students' wok is left 'up in the air'.

When students develop their own questions within a topic, I list specific indidivuals' suggestions on the board and speculate about ways of ordering and connecting them, just as one does in planning a piece of writing. The nature of particular investigations may change; it is the sense that each student's work is a specific contribution to the class exploration of an identified theme which is important, not that the shape of the connections be static.

While groups may consider individual's suggestions before they come to the whole class, it it important to guard against the danger that the groups translate specific suggestions into more generalized questions which diminish the individual voice.

To take an example where I think that happened, Jo-Anne Reid conducted a unit on 'Kids in schools' with a year 9 class.[6] For the second question, which was worded 'What do you want to find out?', rather than 'What do **we** ...', one student, Karen, wrote:

> Here is a list of things which I don't know about school:
> 1. Is it really worth it?
> 2. Do any teachers have nervous breakdowns?
> 3. Would any teacher ever hit a kid in school?
> 4. How often do they clean the toilets?

Karen's list has a personal flavour, which was lost when her group settled on these three questions to investigate:

> How are we marked and graded?
> What does the principal do?
> How important is our schoolwork for getting a job?

My feeling is that Karen's original questions would have prompted more specific and more interesting investigations than the three more processed questions. And I think that students from another group would be more interested in hearing answers to Karen's questions than to the questions decided by her group.

ONGOING ASSESSMENT OF STUDENTS' COMMITMENT TO THE COURSE

Teachers take time to gauge where their students stand in relation to the subject matter, and to have **them** reflect on their position, because they want the students to sense a personal commitment to the work. To maintain that commitment it is also important to introduce fairly regular times for students to reflect, not just on the subject matter, but on how things are going for them generally in the English course. This can be done in a learning record or journal, which can simply be a manilla folder, with two columns like 'What is going well?' and 'What do you want changed or discussed?'.

When students make their own assessments of the course they often blame the teacher, the class or the subject matter for problems they are experiencing. If we have as a goal that students reflect on their work, we have to allow them to make these criticisms because what the students do is intimately linked to these aspects of the classroom context. Many students will only reflect on what they are doing when they see that they might gain someting from it. Thus many will be most involved when they want something changed. If we allow them to evaluate the course, students often then go on to describe their own behaviour as well. In this way, reflection on the course serves as the beginning point for self-assessment, as the following typical examples from learning records indicate.

> I didn't think things were very good when we started but they got better because I like expressing my feelings but I had to adjust because last year I felt really squashed.

> Well at first, I thought what are they asking of me? I can't do this. But the further I went along the more confidence I gained. Sometimes though I have mental blocks and can't seem to write anything and other times I get brainstorms and can't stop writing.

The progression from criticising to reflecting on one's own behaviour is clearest when the students express their responses to very specific aspects of the course. For example, in classes where students are encouraged to express the feelings that are triggered in them,[7] students make statements like this:

> When you set homework on Tuesday night and it is due in on Wednesday, I feel annoyed, because it means I won't spend enough time on it to get satisfaction out of it.

This is an admirable self-assessment because it avoids labelling either the teacher or the student; and describes the self **in context** not in isolation.[8]

Written feedback from students to teacher in a journal or learning record has the advantage that it does not require a lot of class time, but there is the disadvantage that students do not participate in, or even witness, consideration of their reactions. Consequently, regular class discussion of things that are going well and complaints is also important. In these discussions students see that their criticisms are accepted (which means that they express rebellious energy legitimately), they can participate in negotiating solutions to problems that arise, and most importantly, issues are dealt with while they are current.

Students' involvement in reflecting on the curriculum can be further encouraged by allowing them to raise matters for discussion on an agenda sheet posted on the wall. This gives them a way to stimulate a class discussion when **they** see most value in reflecting and expressing their reactions. On the other hand, a commonly used method for getting students' reactions, by questionnaire, is less often successful because it is relatively inflexible and inaccessible to the students. The teacher decides when to hand it out and what the questions are, and even a short questionnaire produces more information than a teacher can quickly acknowledge, let alone act upon.

Ongoing assessment of the students' reactions to the course is part of classroom management. It is particularly important that we work this way when students are rebellious. If instead we impose tasks hurriedly, the students will not, at a later stage, be prepared to reflect on the particulars of their own work, because they won't sense that it is **their** work. It will have been work for the teacher, and therefore it will be the teacher's responsibility to reflect on it.

SOME RESOLUTIONS

Quite often I find myself rushing the introduction of a task, especially when I am anxious about how it will go, or about my relationships with members of that class. Because of my anxiety, I impose the work rather than taking the time to let the students reflect on it and question it, so that I can assess their relationship to it. I forget that sequences of imposed activities, no matter how good they are, 'induce the same sort of numbness and disorientation as watching a whole evening's television'.[9]

So, lately, when I am anxious about a lesson, I take that as a sign that I need to slow down and give more attention to the students. I need to remember that it is the students' learning, not mine; and that I owe it to them to observe courtesies like the following:

1. From time to time, I sould give **advance notice** of activities, explaining why we will be doing them, and how they relate to what we have done before. Discussing what the students might get out of the activities and why these learnings would be important is something of a necessary prerequisite if I want to them to reflect on the worthwhileness of what they are doing.

2. I should introduce tasks of choices on posters or sheets of paper. I can then join the students in reflecting on the tasks. This avoids my having to repeat directions, which apart from being very tiresome, confines me to the role of instructor.

3. When I notice resistance to an activity, I should often focus on that, rather than hoping it will go away. If expression of the resistance does not lead to clarification and greater commitment, I may ask a student if she is prepared to do it anyway. 'I accept you've got that feeling. Would you be prepared to give it a go anyway and see what happens?' Or I may allow a student to sit out, perhaps coming in at his own pace, while getting an undertaking that he will not distract others. Alternatively I may modify the activity, or allow some students to choose an alternative activity or decide to postpone the activity to a later time.

Of course, often a class is ready to work. It will not always be necessary to go slowly in assessing their relationship to the subject matter, for that would be just as insensitive as never to do it.

No doubt there will be times in the future when I rush this process, but I am becoming more aware of how crucial these assessments are and more fascinated with this aspect of teaching, even when it does not go well. I am finding that it is not a question of whether a topic works, but rather **how** it works.

The next chapters (Four to Nine) describe how teachers can help students reflect on their writing, reading and oral language. Chapter Four focuses on the students' ability to reflect on how they go about writing.

4 Helping Students to Reflect on Their Writing Processes

In Chapters One and Two I argued that students' development in writing is often inhibited by the continual threat of a judgemental response from the teacher. Some English teachers reduce the emphasis on **judging** writing, but when judgements are not formally expressed, students still look for them. 'Is this good? Will she like it? Will it have the effect I intended?' These questions are intrinsic to writing. We cannot get rid of judgement altogether.

What we can do is help students describe what they are trying to do when they write, so that they can distance themselves from what they have written — and from any judgements made of it. When a teacher says 'Why did you do that?' or 'I can't understand this part' many students feel they've done the wrong thing, that they've been a bit stupid. If students are to be involved in assessing their own writing, we must help them describe what they are doing when they write. We can help them say things like

'I think I was getting going in this part.'
'At that point I was trying to work out how she'd be feeling.'
'I think I've got something worth developing here.'
'This is the part I thought I could start with.'
'I was trying to find a suitable image there.'
'I thought the reader would want to know that.'

When students can say these things they can reflect on their writing **with** the teacher. They can speak as learners, not delinquent or mistaken children.

In this chapter I refer to six things that writers do:

they get writing going ('I was getting going in this part');

they explore through writing ('At that point I was trying to work out how she'd be feeling');

they make discoveries in writing ('I think I've got something worth developing here');

they choose and reject from what they've written ('This is the part I thought I could start with');

they experiment ('I was trying to find a suitable image there'); and

they anticipate readers' needs ('I thought the reader would want to know that').

These are not six separate steps in the writing process. They overlap and lead into each other during writing.

Each section of this chapter begins with an excerpt from an interview with a secondary school student or students; what they say is, I think, representative of how most students think about their writing. They are usually more concerned with whether it is good or not than with what they are actually doing when they write.

Then I describe briefly what teachers can do with students like these to help them be more articulate when they reflect on their writing process.

I finish each section with excerpts from interviews with year 10 and 11 classes taught by Joy Allen and John Keal at Eudunda Area School. These are much more articulate examples of students talking about what they do when they write.

The interviews that begin and end each section demonstrate ways in which the teacher can assess how students talk about their writing. Although each section focuses on a different aspect of writing, the underlying assessment the teacher is concerned to make is 'Can my students talk about what they are doing when they write? — or do they look to others for the authoritative comments on their work?'

GETTING WRITING GOING

How do you begin a piece of writing?

First of all I just think of what the topic is and try to get an idea in my head of what should happen and then I start to write it down.

If you have to make up the topic, how do you do that?

I don't really, it just comes into my head. I'm sitting there dreaming and it comes in. I might sometimes think of two topics and then I choose the one that's best — or easiest to write on.

Can you think of a time when that happened?

No. It happened a fair while ago.

Has it happened to you that it's time to write, homework maybe, or a deadline is due, and you don't feel like doing any writing? Has that happened?

Well yes. I just force myself. I know I'll be in trouble if I don't.

Should you always do your best writing?

Yes.

There is nothing **wrong** with these typical responses — in this case from a year 10 boy — but I think he would be better equipped if he could refer to specific ways he had been able to generate writing, and alternative topics for writing, when he was finding it difficult to get started. As it is he seems to be at the mercy of a good topic or a fluke of inspiration.

Getting started is a common problem, either because students are anxious about whether their writing will be good or because they already expect that it will not be up to standard. When writing is provoking anxiety, a basic strategy for getting started is to temporarily drop one's standards. Learning about writing involves learning to do that. So if my students are not writing freely and willingly, I need to make sure that they do not think they always have to do their best work, for that represents a continual trial and not a climate for learning. I do want them to care about what they're doing, but not to expect high quality of themselves at every step along the way.

For getting writing started, I have found Moffett's suggestion of going from stream of consciousness writing to spontaneous jottings of sensory impressions, memories and thoughts very useful. These tasks come very easily to students. His account[1] of these procedures is concise and practical, so there is no need to summarize it here, but it is worthwhile to emphasize the multiple purposes which he outlines for stream of consciousness writing:

(1) to limber up the student and make his writing fluent and natural;

(2) to show him that there is plenty to write about if he just becomes aware of what is going on in and around him;

(3) to anchor writing in honest, original interaction between him and the world; and

(4) to provide a sampling of his own verbalization which he may subsequently examine to learn about the putting of things into words.[2]

Terms which Moffett uses, like stream of consciousness, monologue and inner speech, are readily remembered by students when they are experiencing these processes.

A similar approach is 'freewriting', described in Peter Elbow's *Writing without teachers*[3] and *Writing with power*[4], and by Ken Macrorie, with these instructions, in *Searching writing*:

For twelve minutes write as fast as you can whatever comes to mind. Don't worry about spelling, punctuation, or grammar, or what you think a teacher might want you to say. Write as fast as you can and still be legible. Don't stop. If at any point, you can't think of what to write, look in front of you — at the wall, window, ceiling, whatever — and start describing what you see. You'll find you're soon thinking yourself into a chain of sentences that belong to you. Say to yourself, 'What goes down here is going to be truth of some kind, nothing phony, nothing designed to make me look good'.[5]

Similarly, students can begin writing by **brainstorming**[6] specific words, ideas and phrases which relate to a topic — or may lead to one. For example, in approaching a question on *Macbeth*, students can brainstorm everything they think might be relevant; incidents, interpretations, associations and judgements. Later it may be appropriate for them to separate these elements. This can be done individually and it is also a valuable and clearly defined group task.

Journal writing which is not graded by the teacher, and often not even seen, is a common approach to tackling the problem of students' reluctance to write; but the more specific exercises described here are valuable because during them a class or small group can discuss a writing experience which they have had in common.

When students have experienced different ways of getting started, they can talk articulately about how they begin. Hopefully, in the future, when they are finding writing difficult, they will be able to say to themselves 'I am having trouble getting going, but I know a few ways of handling that'. Here are year 10 and 11 students talking about how they begin writing.

How do you begin a piece of writing?

Sonia: We had a real object there and we just looked at it and thought about it and you just got these thoughts coming to you. Lots of questions. Why is it like this? Why is it blue? Why is it scratched? Who scratched it? And then you sort of try and answer the questions as best you can. You look at it and you send these ideas out to it and they come back better. You bounce them off the thing.

Pam: If I make a picture in my head then I know what I want to write.

Greg: We studied *'To Kill a Mockingbird'* and we had to write about Atticus. If you could just see yourself in his place, it's easier to write, because I reckon I could write an essay about myself.

Lisa: I wasn't thinking hard what I wanted to write, just letting thoughts flow through. But you had to concentrate because someone would open the door and come bursting into the classroom. I thought I'd let things come to my mind, smells and tastes and things like that.

During my holidays I went to Queensland and there's this really nice place. I could feel myself being there with all the quietness. I could actually hear the waterfall coming down and making all the splashing noises and it was a real tropical area with lots of rain-forest trees and the sun was shining and you could feel that humid, sultry bit and I could actually feel that. It all came to me. I was there again, where I was during the holidays. It was really good.

Then I just started writing as something came to my mind and I just kept going. I didn't keep all my ideas. They weren't in any order, they just kept coming out. When we had to do drafts I organized all the thoughts into paragraphs and things like that.

At first I didn't put commas in, just phrases, some sentences, occasionally just words.

Angele: I was doodling and I saw the lines and I was looking at the desk and I could see shadows. Then some of my doodling was like shadows destroying the lines, and I wrote a bit and it didn't seem right, but I'd got the bit about the shadows destroying the lines down.

EXPLORING THROUGH WRITING

Many students see writing as simply transcribing what they should have got clear before they began to write. Once you've begun to write, it should all come out 'right'! The year 10 boy, quoted earlier, seemed to understand writing in this way.

When you start writing, do you know where you are headed?

Yes, because we've been taught to stay on the one subject and not to go off into other places. You just stay on that one person or thing that you are talking about.

What if you're writing about something and you find you don't really know enough about it? Does that ever happen?

No, it doesn't. We're never given topics that don't have enough information.

In *Coming on Centre*, Moffett argues that 'so much of the dullness, awkwardness, shallowness and opacity that teachers object to in student writing owes to skimming along in the froth instead of plunging into the current, where intuition lines up with intelligence and particularities of experience correct for cliché.[7]

I found that year 9 students readily accepted that much of our thought is at a relatively superficial level; rather like quacking or chattering at the level of 'How-are-you-going? O.K.-thanks. How-are-you? Have-a-good-weekend'. Easy come, easy go. There are deeper, more personal levels of experience and verbalization than these ('What you are really thinking and feeling when you say "Not-bad-how-are-you?"').

It is important that students be aware of and able to use language at both these levels. So when students have produced writing which seemed to be largely determined by television or Mills and Boon, when the language was colourless, or the wording conveyed the impression that they knew little about what they were writing, I've talked to them about different levels of experience and used simple relaxation techniques to encourage a more personal engagement in writing.

Joy Allen talks to her classes about how 'we tend to block inner speech a lot. And yet what comes from there tends to be more powerful, more honest.' When I asked if the students resisted this idea, Joy replied: 'No. I say "Remember when you were doing stream of consciousness — it was as if you were in touch with a voice inside of you, wasn't it?" And there is a general corroboration of that. They recognise it.'

At other times I have used a more discursive strategy of asking the students to pick the strongest part of a stream of consciousness or journal entry and to write associations to that. Or students can write about the most surprising or unusual element in a brainstorm. By getting them to go into further exploration of a specific utterance, we are encouraging deeper reflection. We are much less likely to get language that is simply an echo of other people's words.

Another strategy is for students to write in the role of a character or object. Drama is useful to introduce this and simple, symbolic props can help elicit belief in this process of empathising with the characters or objects. I find myself suggesting, 'You have all these roles within you. Let's explore them'.

When students use methods like these to explore in their writing, they find it more exciting and teachers do too. Some of the Eudunda Area School students described exploring they had done:

When you start writing, do you know where you are headed?

Lisa: I write like mad. One night a thought came to me in bed and I thought 'That's good,' and I just kept writing and writing. I wrote about God and I almost talked myself out of believing in Him, with just the questions I thought about.

Sonia: Sometimes, but not always. Like I did a spontaneous reflective monologue on death. I didn't know much about it. I came up with these ideas I'd never have thought of if I hadn't done this reflective thing. Some of the ideas you get are really great. Some are not so great. If you get your mind blank and then you look at something, you think about it completely differently. You've got it there! I used a person sitting scross from me. His life. I was doing death. I thought — 'What's going to happen when he dies?' Ideas just seemed to come from nowhere, they just floated in by themselves. It sounds funny, but that's what happens.

What if you're writing about someting and you find you don't really know enough about it? Does that ever happen?

Lyn: What that happens to me I go back to my jottings and I choose a different topic.

DISCOVERING

When students see writing as a display of one's knowledge, put on for a judge, they often do not understand that writing can lead us to new uderstandings. The year 10 boy I interviewed had not had this experience:

Can you remember making any discoveries as you were writing?

How do you mean discoveries?

Well maybe you're writing away, and then you think, 'Oh gosh, I'd never thought of it quite that way before'.

No.

Does the writing ever spring surprises on you? Do you ever think, 'Gosh, look at that!?'

No.

When you're writing do you sometimes look at the different ideas you've expressed and think, 'Hey! they're connected together in ways I hadn't thought of till I did that piece of writing?

No.

Do you learn anything through writing?

Yes. Most of the kids in our class, they find the English essays that we receive boring and they can't quite cope with them and they don't want to do them at all. But I find that I enjoy them because I learn more. If I get corrections I learn what I've done wrong. That's what I like about the essays. You get to learn things: mistakes like punctuation. My content is good. Next time there's less chance of having another mistake. Hopefully one day I'll get one that doesn't have any mistakes. But that's doubtful.

When students write more freely, they discover that a wide range of ideas, sensations and feelings appear in what they write. For some, seeing how many words they have been able to get down will be an important discovery. Moffett[8] suggests getting students to record the contents of stream of consciousness in terms of sensations, memories, emotions, fantasies and reflections. Marissa Wilkins, a teacher at Adelaide High School, gets year 9 students to keep an index to their writing journals. For each entry they record its content, form, purpose, type of discource, audience and how they feel about it. The terms for describing form, purpose and type of discourse are discussed in class and made into charts for the students to refer to. As the year goes on, Marissa encourages them to experiment with new forms, purposes, audiences and so on.

Lyn Wilkinson, at Mawson High School, got students to look through their first brainstormed lists of 'people, events and things which are significant for you', to find 'bits that surprised you — or something you haven't thought of in a long time...' She discussed how the students responded:

The Year 11's picked that up pretty well straight away. The Year 8's didn't. I had to take a long time over it with the Year 8's.

I read this in Graves.[9] Listen, it's beautiful! 'The craftsperson looks for differences in the material, the surprise, the explosion that will set him aback. Surprises are friends, not enemies. Surprises mean changes, whole new arrangements, new ways to revise, reform, reshape'.

This was exactly what we were talking about in class. I think the biggest problem with kids' writing in school is that it lacks this. When I was writing with the kids, in my list of memories, I'd start off with something that was fairly clear in my memory, and gradually you sort of go backwards into things that are very vague and unclear and then suddenly you go bang! You think Oooh! I haven't thought of that for such a long time! And you think, 'It's strange that I'd almost forgotten it, and it's taken all this effort to remember it, but when I did remember it I got this sort of Oooh! feeling? You think 'Gee!' And I think that's what makes it worth writing about.

It's like with academic stuff when you read someting or you suddenly write a sentence and you think 'Oh! That encapsulates, after all this time, exactly what I've been on about'. It's terrific!

I think you need that feeling of Oooh! to make it worth writing. And the kid can go on and validate that experience and make sense of it and maybe use it, embroider it; try to do something a bit different with the experience, so it makes sense to other people.

Now that is what the kids were doing. I remember one kid, they were building a new room on their house and how he'd got there was I'd set them a speed writing exercise on weather. He was telling about the winter and how difficult it made building and he got onto talking about this new room and obviously it was important to him because it was big family thing. They were all working on it together. They'd all planned it together and then it was stuffing them all up together, because it was pouring rain and the new room was getting full of water. If I had set the topic, he wouldn't have written with the same sense of enjoyment or exploration or recreation.'

Many students will only open up to making discoveries in their writing when they can remove the straight-jacket of their expectation that writing and thinking should come in a predictable, linear sequence.

To get discovering going will require both more raw, unprocessed material, like the brainstoms done by the students in Lyn Wilkinson's classes, and reflection on that material. When a student finds a 'gold nugget' to show around, the motivation will be stronger to practise techniques for polishing it.

And as Moffett has argued,[10] 'What really teaches composition — putting together — is disorder. Clarity and objectivity become learning challenges only when content and form are **not** given to the learner but when he must find and forge his own from his inchoate thought. Now, **that's** hard.'

When students make discoveries as they write they get a satisfaction which is their own: they are not dependent on others for approval and reward...

Can you remember making any discoveries as you were writing?

Sonia: I did this story on a girl who gets on drugs and I started with her parents. She got hooked on drugs because of her parents' problems, and then *her* children will probably have problems, unless she gets out of this drugs thing. Like your problems are sometimes created by yourself, but they can be created by somebody else and it can be pushed down onto you and then you push it down onto somebody else.
          Before I'd just thought that people created their own problems, but it's not always that way. Sometimes people try really hard and they still get problems they don't want.

Jane: I wrote about being my best friend and I thought 'Gosh I'd have to live in her house, eat the food *she* eats. I'd have to do all the things she does and I thought, 'Oh, I'm glad I'm me!'

Does the writing ever spring surprises on you?

Angele: I've never put two ideas like that to make a poem before: two new ideas. Before I'd written more simple things. I don't quite know why I said the lines and the shadows compete. I wouldn't have said they compete, but it felt right at the time.

CHOOSING AND REJECTING

Many students see a piece of writing as a fixed thing. Apart from correcting errors, it is left as it is. It's difficult to talk to students about how they evaluate their work if it's all good enough!...

Say you've been preparing something and you decide not to put part of what you've written in the final copy; does that happen?

Well, maybe with a line of writing, but no more than that. Nothing more than a sentence. But I don't usually have to leave anything out.

Have you ever started to write something and then you gave up on it because it was not going how you wanted it to — and started again another time?

No. I've always planned my idea and just thought about it as to what would be best. I've already got what would be the best to write on, the most exciting, and I just go.

When students are prepared to delete whole passages from their writing 'it means that they're prepared to evaluate their own writing and that they've got a clear idea of what they want'.[11] It is through this selection, that they develop a sense of the value of their writing.

After discussing discovering in writing, Lyn Wilkinson went on to describe the importance of students choosing and rejecting.

The kid who stands out in a class who writes on 'My Holiday', is the kid who breaks the accepted rules and *chooses* just one little, minute incident that happened in the holidays and writes a whole story about it. They're the ones that the teacher pulls out and says 'These are good. They have written about the topic well. Ironically, these kids have not done what the teacher asked. They have defined the task much more narrowly. And they get rewarded for it?

Also kids often think that once they've started writing they're locked in. Secondary kids think that every problem has to be solved as you go along. So you have to start with a good opening sentence which starts with a capital letter and ends with a full stop and your first paragraph has to be consistent. And then you take one of those ideas and begin your second paragraph and so on. One of the things you can learn is, 'I'll scrap it. I'll do something different. None of that is relevant. I'm going to use this bit here as my beginning'.

I want them to be aware of this kind of thinking so I show them examples of it from my writing. I want them to know they've got something to say and they can manipulate it.

Maybe poor writers don't let themselves fiddle around enough, explore enough different alternatives. They think once they've thought of an alternative that has to be the one they use.

After all, most of us were taught that good writers know where it's going to go before they write.

As well as demonstrating choosing and rejecting in relation to her own writing, the teacher can get students to practise it by asking them to read favourite paragraphs — sometimes from their writing, sometimes from what they've read. Students can also be required to choose **some** of their first drafts for redrafting and polishing, while leaving others aside. We should not force them to redraft all their work, if they would rather reject some of it. Finally, a **small selection** of writing should be required for publication or for grading by an external judge (see Chapter Ten); this makes the students reflect upon the value of their work and, with the teacher's help, choose what they think is best.

When students, like those interviewed at Eudunda Area School, are used to choosing and rejecting, they are more in control of their writing. They can separate themselves from it and evaluate it, rather than see writing as a situation in which they are always on trial.

> *Say you've been preparing something and you decide not to put part of what you've written in the final copy. Does that happen?*

Greg: Sometimes I think some idea is really good. It's one of my best ideas but it doesn't fit in with all the other ideas when I'm writing, so it just gets left out.

Lisa: Bits I leave out come from all over the place.

Jane: I've taken out whole paragraphs.

> *Have you ever started to write something and then you gave up on it because it was not going how you wanted it to, and started again another time?*

Jane: I was doing an essay in the exam. I wrote this whole essay and I looked at it and I said 'that stinks'! So I turned around and started again. The second piece was better.

Tim: You can just throw away your first draft and then rewrite it. It turns out better than the first. You can't really remember how you did it before, but you put it into different words.

EXPERIMENTING

I suggested in the first chapter that students often cannot explain how they are experimenting in English. The following examples come from year 10 and 11 students. They are more articulate than the typical response and indicate why students avoid experimenting ....

Can you remember experimenting in your writing?

I haven't and wouldn't experiment with writing at all, because I only write for the teacher and if the teacher likes what I'm doing already, I might as well keep on doing the same thing.

I wouldn't dare. I think it's partly because I don't know what is new, or I don't know that there is something different around, and also because I'm scared of how it's going to turn out. I'm not sure if it's going to be good or bad. I'm just not confident enough.

Yes. At the beginning of high school, when I wasn't quite as experienced as I am now. I kind of practised and did lots of funny things. But now, I don't seem to really want to. I just want to get it over and done with I enjoy doing most of it. It's just it's best to get it out of the way.

Can you remember any of these experiments? What you were trying?

No. It's too far back.

Can you think of something you've tried that didn't work in your writing?

Never. They've always worked.

When students are not conscious of their experiments, our comments on their work are largely wasted, because the interaction is too one-sided. We end up trying to inject our articulate language into the students: but to them, terms like contrast, specificity, colourful language, are just words. Until the students have **consciously** manipulated these things, their learning of those terms is not grounded in their own experience.

Steve Dowdy of Ingle Farm High School found that his year 8 students had little sense of what they were experimenting with — or even what they were able to do in their writing. So he carefully set about making sure they got an experience of experimenting — and they were the students' experiments, not his. I have found that adults enjoy this procedure. It is worth describing in some detail.

The class was given a week to settle on a piece of writing they thought showed quality. Most chose a passage from a novel read in class (e.g. *Half days and patched pants* by Max Colwell), a fragment from a short story (e.g. Henry Lawson) or something from a magazine (e.g. an advertisement form *National Geographic*).

Then over two weeks each student read an extract to the class and explained what it was that made it a piece of quality writing. Other students commented on other parts of the extract, or said 'That's like mine…. Can I do mine now?' Some drew parallels with other things the class had read. Many of the extracts were humorous and Banjo Patterson's short story, *The Lobster and the Lioness*, was often referred to.

The class then drew up a poster headed 'Good writing may include'. Each student wrote down characteristics of their chosen piece, in a bright colour. The poster was displayed on the wall for the rest of the year.

GOOD WRITING *MAY* INCLUDE

Exaggeration
Accurate
punctuation
Comparisons
Puns

Humour
Creativity
Originality
Imagery
Personification

Using a Thesaurus
to use different
adjectives!
Accurate spelling
Fully describe
   characters
Keep the story
   m-o-v-i-n-g
Use a beginning
which attracts
attention
Use a twist at the
end

Vary the beginning
of sentences

Use all 5 senses

Yarns

Definite beginning,
middle and end!

Paragraphs

PLAN AHEAD

Similes — a simile is a
comparison using like
or as to link the two
items

Metaphors — a
metaphor is a
comparison in which
you give the qualities of
one thing to another,
e.g. She is a pig.

A point to the story

Contrasts

Edit and redraft to
correct errors and to
improve ideas

Use an interesting title

Then the students had to write a short piece experimenting with one of these characteristics. When they were ready, they read their work to the class and explained what it was they were trying to do. Each student was happy to do it. If a student referred only to the content of his/her writing (e.g. 'This is good because Fords are better than Holdens'), Steve would ask

But what are you doing?

Putting one against the other.

What's a word for that?

Contrast.

He drew their attention to formal terms for what they had done, so that they could recognize the technique and consciously use it again, to achieve a similar effect.

These experiments were pinned on the wall alongside the 'Good writing may include' poter. In a few cases it was difficult to understand what was being attempted. For example, in the following piece Katrina was experimenting with humour:

THE RIDE

It was a quiet night with a full moon. I had just been kindapped while getting clothes off the clothesline. A bag had been shoved over my head, and I couldn't see a thing. I was shoved into a marone car with a 4.2 engine. The car was a commodore with 8 cylinders. It had red velvet seats and the outside was marone. We were travelling towards the city. We stopped at the main entrance of the royal show. They took the bag off my head and pushed me into the Mad Mouse. I had never been so scared in my life. I asked them why it was the Mad Mouse and not another ride. They said 'We just want to see if our ride was in good condition'. They took me home. I asked them to come in for a cup of tea, but they said they were in a hurry, otherwise they would have come in and met my parents.

Katrina Greenshields

In most cases it was easier to see what the writer was trying:

AN EXAMPLE OF GOOD WRITING

A spooky noise brought me back to earth, and whereas I was dreaming of flying in space, I now had to face reality. Creak went something behind me. I turned and it was the door opening a fraction. A sliver of light streamed in and I saw a white shape in the doorway. Now there was no noise and this made it even more scarier. I sat still terrified into inaction until someone said 'Trick or Treat'.

Anthony Steel

Anthony was experimenting with 'a twist at the end'.

The jungle of possible
DEATH

While walking through a desolated jungle, in the very heart of Africa, I heard a spine tingling noise. My heart thumped like the natives banging on their drums, and my body tingled like I was laying on a bed of nails. As I took a step forward, the noise got louder. My brain was whirling like a computer and I was trying to work out what it was.

It would be a head hunter, a cannibal, a fierce lion or tiger or something like that. I decided to find out, but as I moved closer, BANG!

A twenty foot monster jumped out and shot a 3 foot bullet at me. Luckily it missed.

I ran at 350 miles an hour until 2 hours later, I came to a village where I was taken home.

Julie Gwatking

Julie's experiment was to use exaggeration.

GOOD WRITING

A flash of lightning struck the ground outback once, and started a
20-mile-an-hour grass fire.

  I was just about to make some tea, so I decided to hold me billy over the
flames.

  Talk about stiff! I had to chase that fire for 10 miles before me billy
came to the boil.

  … And then I discovered I'd left me tea behind.

Hamish Foweraker

Hamish's experiment was 'to tell a yarn'.

Experimenting with forms is a powerful way to extend students' power
over language. In addition, in these exercises, we can see how students
enjoy playing around with words.

Following this the students were to prepare a new piece of quality
writing for an external judge. It was during this time that I began visiting
the class and I found that these year 8s were more articulate than most
older classes when it came to describing what they were trying to do in
their writing.

Hamish: 'I think it's interesting and funny. I've used lots of exaggeration — and similes' (showning specific examples).

Julie: 'I think this is quality writing because I've got good
descriptions — the dragon's eyes, the cottage. You can get an
image in your mind. When I write it, it's as though I can smell
the cottage — it's musty and old.'

Quite a few students referred explicitly to the 'Good writing may
include' poster to explain how their work showed quality. As Katrina
said:

It's easy to see what you can try to get in a piece of quality writing, because
you can just look up at the sheet. You don't have to ask the teacher. It's
not cheating because you're the person who created that sheet up there.
They use our ideas and we use theirs. You've got more of a choice as to
what to write in your story.

Steve explained how the 'Good writing may include' poster gets
added to as the year goes on.

'Use all five senses'. That was added to the chart later. We were talking
about how we could improve the stories. Some kids said you could show
what it looked or felt like. I focussed on that. We talked about all the five
senses and how they can be used in a piece of writing. Katrina seemed to
be particularly interested in it, so I told her to put it up on the chart. For a
while she was the resident expert on it.'

Many students will feel most secure when we provide them with a form or model from which they can improvise. Then they are not overwhelmed by the choices open to them — and have a chance of conceptualizing what specifically they are trying.

Experienced writers and readers know the structure of, for example, stories, so they can play with interrupting routines, reincorporating characters and building up tension. Less experienced students can be shown how to experiment with elements like these. What Steve did is powerful because it led the students to their own experiments. Having had that experience, the students were more aware of experimenting as a process in learning writing. They could also speak more authoritatively about their writing and were more willing to engage in experiments suggested by the teacher.

Given the importance of students knowing how they are experimenting in their writing, it is a pity that so few can talk in these terms. Some of the students at Eudunda Area School could do so:

> *Can you remember experimenting in your writing?*

Tim: I was home. I had the flu and I read *The Man From Snowy River*, which I was given for my birthday. I was interested in it and I started writing. I copied it. I wrote in ballad form. It worked out all right. It was quite interesting.

Greg: Last year I was in one of those moods where I felt like mucking around. I started writing this story. I was so relaxed. These real weird and good ideas came out and I finished up writing this story which was so way-out. There was someting about a bionic kangaroo and wombats and Russians ...

Lisa: I did one thing about childhood memories, but then I made it into a story. Mrs. Allen said there was this lady writing stories from her childhood experiences, and they were like stories. I wouldn't have believed that she wrote them from her own experiences. I tried to do something similar to that. It worked out a lot better.

ANTICIPATING READERS' NEEDS

Writers cannot include every possible perspective, every qualification, every subtlety. You have to choose a position and say it is (or was) like this, when there are a myriad of ways of seeing and saying things.

Reflecting on which of different possible meanings you will express is fundamental writing; it is the most rigorous reflective process a writer must confront. But the sad fact is that students in schools and higher education rarely speculate with their teachers about what they will get across to the reader:

Can you remember making changes to a piece of writing to make it more appealing to the reader?

Not very often. But occasionally I read it again and I find it becomes very boring. Like I go into too much detail. So I have to change it.

What sort of changes?

I don't know. I can't really think about it.

How do you decide how the reader is likely to react?

I get other kids in the class to read my writing. I usually go by their judgement. But not all the time. I go by my ideas. I don't really listen to what they say.
They say my stories are 'interesting', 'enjoyable', but not 'fantasitc'. The teacher usually says my content is 'good'.

A massive neglect in the area of students anticipating readers' needs comes about because, in most classrooms, the teacher assesses the value of the writing, often in terms of a grade or a mark. When the teacher is the only reader whose response actually **counts**, there is simply no call for a reflective discussion which considers how readers **might** react; the teacher can simply say what his response is. In this situatioin many students are only concerned to find out from the teacher what the rules of the game are. Meaningful engagement, where the student actively imagines the audience's needs, only happens when the student cares more about the writing than doing well at school; or when the teacher organizes judgemental assessment in such a way that it does not lock him into being the judge (see Chapters Ten to Thirteen).

Good English teachers also organize it so that students help each other reflect on the readers' needs. Her is how Lola Brown did it:

> I said they had to write about something they experienced today, when they were at home this evening, and to do that every night for the next two weeks. To show them what I meant, I told them about my yesterday....
>
> Next day, they brought in their writing. I spent ten minutes illustrating what I meant by 'being specific'; how 'I saw the tree in the paddock' leaves the reader floundering; he can't get hold of the picture in the writer's mind. He has too many questions. What tree? What shape? Bare? Covered with leaves?
>
> I asked them to pair off, fasten on a sentence in each other's work and be the reader: ask the questions. Then, as the writer, add the necessary detail that answers them.[12]

I have found it useful to get writers to include the details asked for, as an experiment, even if they feel that the writing will not be improved: to do it and then reflect on whether it improves the writing. It is this manipulation and reflection on writing that we want students to learn. It does not matter if their revisions do not always produce a better product.

Lola continued:

Next we focussed on 'grabbing the reader's attention'. I read them the first sentence of an article I'd recently written: 'They sit there, the pen-chewers, faces blank, minds numb in anticipation of another experience of self-exposure from which there is no escape.' Then I read them the opening of the third paragraph in it: 'In 1976 I was one of a group of teachers at the Elizabeth High School...' I asked them why one was a better beginning.

They told me. More dramatic; has the reader puzzled and guessing because it's indirect, and, as I translated it, because it lifts the reader out of his armchair, away from his desk into *my* world, the one I want him to explore.

Then they took the first sentence from last night's writing and re-wrote it. And they really had understood. Perhaps it was a gimmick, a formula. But if it was, it gave them the sense of having taken a step forward in writing. Of that, I was sure. Often, all they did was to eliminate an inessential phrase or clause from the beginning. 'On the way home from school I crossed the bridge...' simply had its opening phrase chopped off, and the changed impact was obvious to everybody. We went on to predict what each piece was about.

After lessons like this, wall charts can be made which list questions for students to ask of their writing. For example,

What parts are particularly strong?
Which parts are weak?
Is there information here which the reader doesn't need to be told?
What does the reader need to know more about?
Does your beginning grab the reader's attention?

For these charts to be used effectively, the questions must emphasize how the work **will be read**, and the students need to have experienced using the questions, one at a time, in class work.

Here is an example of a student explaining how she worked on a poem to give the reader a more accurate picture of what she was describing.

Can you remember making changes to a piece of writing to make it more appealing to the reader?

Lisa: I did that with this poem: I was sure readers wouldn't be interested in it.

> The Kondalilla Falls,
>   Rushing, gushing water.
>   A tiny paradise hidden
>   in a rain forest. A
>   beautiful sight after

a journey through tall,
   never-ending trees. You
      feel like an ant. It is
         cool and refreshing and
            well worth the 8km walk.

So I wrote down my impressions of the place: 'crashing water, thundering water, rotting wood smells, damp underfoot, narrow winding paths, steep ascents, and so on. After a lot of fiddling around, I was describing it more — and I had a slightly different style. I'd thought about it a lot more.

The Kondalilla Falls
I've walked more than 2 kilometres
Through a dense, tropical rainforest
Giant, never-ending trees,
Block out the sun's warmth
Following winding, narrow paths
Conquering steep ascents
A hidden paradise is revealed
A calm stream of water
Flows helplessly towards the edge
of a cliff
Suddenly its journey begins
Crashing over slimey rocks
Gushing into huge boulders
Splashing and rushing to the bottom
of the falls
Suddenly
as it began
it ends
Returning to a calm stream
of water.

The activities described so briefly in this chapter are designed to help students think about how they go about writing and rewriting. Some teachers require students to give an account of how they developed a piece from rough draft to final copy. These accounts can be written, spoken onto a tape or shared in a discussion with the teacher and other students.

Where students report that their writing comes easily, they may not have a lot to say about their writing process; but regardless of how smoothly these students write, they can still be asked to give an account of how they have **experimented** in writing during the year, for conceptualising these experiments will be an important part of learning, even for writers who work intuitively much of the time.

The next chapter also focuses on writing. It describes strategies for helping students reflect on pieces of writing, be they drafts or finished products.

5 Helping Students Become Better Readers of Their Own Writing

MONITORING THE STUDENT'S ENGAGEMENT WITH A PIECE OF WRITING

Donald Murray[1] has emphasized that when we comment on a student's writing, we are talking to another reader of the writing — the writer's 'other self': for the principal goal of commenting should be to educate the student's reading of his or her own work. It is not education if students simply tack our improvements onto their writing without haveing read to see whether the change is called for.

It seems obvious that there is little point making detailed comments on students' writing if they have largely forgotten it, or are thinking about something else at the time. Even so, in the rush that is school life, I often talk to students about their writing, **assuming** that it is fresh in their memory or that they will read it again, which means that much of this effort is wasted. There is a safeguard against this and that is to **start** by asking the students to answer one or more of the following questions:

- What is the most important thing you're saying?
- Why is this piece of writing important?
- What will the reader get out of it?
- Which part do you feel closest to?
- Which part do you most want a reaction to?
- Which part are you least happy with?

and if you've seen the piece in an earlier draft,

● Did you make any changes? Does it read better now?

It is a good idea to display these questions on a poster in the classroom. Doing so helps the students get used to them and sometimes they suggest the question they consider most relevant.

These questions require the writer to be a reader of the piece. They also allow the teacher to assess how engaged that student is with it.

If the student indicates concern about the writing, then we can spend more time on the piece than we would if it appears to be over and done with. As well, what the student says can guide us to concentrate on those aspects of the writing which the student most wants comments on.

When the student begins by telling us how she reads her work, then we can be quite direct in our response. We can indicate that we read it differently, or we can offer suggestions. We can respond freely and naturally. It is important not to be too cautious and non-directive, for that can sap the teacher and student of energy. This is demonstrated in the following interaction involving a teacher who felt that she should avoid expressing her own reactions directly (she disliked the student's piece), and that she should respond as she thought a counsellor would.

Teacher: Judy, it seems to me, from your piece of writing, you really enjoyed yourself at Goolwa.

Judy: Yeah, it was really good.

Teacher: Were some things at Goolwa better than others?

Judy: Oh yeah, the nights were really good.

Teacher: Would it be important to mention that?

Judy: Yes, I suppose.

Teacher: (long pause) .... Why?

Judy: Ah well, I should have put it in.

Teacher: Why do you think you should have put it in?

Judy: I'm trying to put down what happened.

Teacher: O.K., but you've only talked about one night. Would it be more interesting to talk about the other nights? Are you going to do that?

Judy: Yes.

Teacher: That'd be good. One thing; 'trick' is that the most appropriate word? ... What did you mean by tricks?

Judy: I could, um, I suppose, they're interesting things. I could imagine doing them.

Teacher: So tricks is O.K. to use?

Judy: Perhaps, sounds as though it gives you the wrong meaning. Yeah, I'll find another word. I'd already used ideas twice.

Teacher: So you say you wanted variety. Can you use a Thesaurus?

Judy: Yes, yes perhaps I could look in it.

Teacher: Is there anything else you want to change or alter?

Judy: No, not that I can think of at the moment.

Teacher: You've got some ideas to work on there, so how about you go away and play around with them a bit and if you've got any problems talk to one of the others or come back and talk to me.

If we are as indirect as this, we'll become very tired and our students will probably end up thinking that we didn't like their work but couldn't bring ourselves to deliver the verdict directly.

Why would a teacher be so indirect? Teachers sometimes feel that they must treat a student's work with kid gloves, so as to show respect for the student. They talk of students being damaged by challenging comments. But students' motivation to work is damaged by interactions like the one just quoted: a lack of integrity in the teacher's response stimulates a similar lack of integrity in a student who agrees to revise work, but in fact has little interest in doing so. We can more effectively show respect for students by having high expectations of them; not treating them as if they are in danger of falling to bits on the floor — and by treating their work **seriously** (as discussed in the next section).

Another reason why teachers often avoid suggesting improvements to students is that they fear that the students may include any suggestions they make, merely to gain a better grade. And when a student does include the teacher's suggestions, it is very difficult for the teacher then to turn around and give the work a low grade. Teachers often admit to giving higher grades to students who follow their advice. This can have the effect of encouraging students to accept advice uncritically.

The solution to this problem should not be to avoid giving help. Rather, grading should be avoided and if on occasions it is required and the criteria have not been clearly specified, then it should be done by someone other than the classroom teacher (see Chapters Ten to Fourteen for procedures which reduce the emphasis on grading). Then students know that, while the class teacher's advice usually merits consideration, it is not an automatic short cut to a higher grade.

We should organize grading this way, so that we are free to express **our** concern that the students' work be of high quality, in a practical, concrete way. We must be free to say 'Here are a couple of things you might do. Try them, as experiments, even if you don't like the ideas at first, and then decide which reads best and is closest to what you want to say.'

What of students who do not have answers to any of the questions listed on p. 51–2? It is often appropriate to ask them to read through their work again to find an answer to **one** of them. If some persist in not having answers, it may not be worthwhile to spend a lot of time commenting on it.

However there will be some whose eagerness tells you that they are focused on getting a response from you as a reader of the piece, not as a teacher. Their attitude might be 'Tell me what you think of it. I don't want to say anything to you until you've read it.' If they want you to respond unaffected by what they could tell you about the writing, that is quite legitimate, and I consider this type of response in the next two sections.

SHOWING HOW YOU READ

The acid test of the effectiveness of a piece of writing is whether it affects the reader as the writer intended; but often teachers do not feel free to say when a piece has failed in that way. They feel much more responsible for the students' work.

Helen Richardson, a teacher at Elizabeth High School, said to me recently, 'There are times when I look at a piece of work and I think, "I'm an English teacher! Surely I can find two things this kid needs to learn, that will help him with future pieces." Yet sometimes I can't.'

Like Helen, most English teachers feel a responsibility to comment in a way that will prompt improvement in future pieces. Consequently, the task of reading students' work is a highly stressful one, not because it is difficult to read, but because it is difficult to work out the comment one **should** make. It should simultaneously encourage, recognise, correct and instruct. Faced with that pressure, marking is very hard work that can be fiercely resented, especially when the teacher has a nagging suspicion that the time is largely wasted; that the comments won't be useful.

Because teachers feel a responsibility to conceptualize the whole piece of writing and to see patterns which indicate what help is needed, they often end up making only vague, general comments. Is there a less demanding role for the teacher, one which relies more on simply reading what students write, and less on processing an overall perspective and agonizing over the writing of the comment? If there were, could such a response be instructive? And could students be taught to respond as more articulate readers?

These questions can be answered positively: and the key is to switch the focus from an overall comment, to the specifics of reading the students' writing.

Here is the first part of a story written by David, a year 9 boy. At home one night, I read the whole of his story aloud, dramatically, onto a cassette tape. As I read I interrupted my reading to comment on my experience as a reader of the piece. The comments which I made during the first part of the story are indicated in italics.

OF AN UNMENTIONABLE THING

Though I hate to dare admit it. It did happen. I didn't know what was happening then and I still don't know now. All I know is that it was terrifying.

O.K., first paragraph short. Short sentences got me very interested. It's very easy to understand and you've implied that it will be hard to believe what I'm going to read, and that it was confusing to you and that you still haven't put it together, but that it was terrifying. So I'm looking forward now to reading the second paragraph.

I think it started off in a dark, dingy, smoke-ridden cellar. This cellar was used as a sort of bar, but it was virtually unknown, and few of those who knew it did not shun it. I was there in search of a story for my paper. Neither me nor my editor knew what the story I was after was about, but in this area lately there had been many reports of something that prowled the dark lanes and alleys bringing great fear and a feeling of evil and doom. No-one knew what shape this evil took. Most who had encountered it said they had felt its presence of doom, and seen an indistinct blur. It was always encountered at night in dark alleys or lanes.

That's good atmosphere there. 'I think' seems a bit weak but, again, I'm not sure. It's adding that little bit of uncertainty.

'Few of those who knew it did not shun it'. In other words, most of those who knew it did shun it. Right, that's the effect it had on me at first.

I was sitting in the bar hoping that someting might happen like the arrival of an unusual customer, but all customers, bar myself, were unusual! Like the bar tender, the few customers were fairly short and heavily built, all their movments seemed clumsy and they spoke in

Great! This is very sustained, casting a lot of ominous questions in my mind … Right.

That's a good joke.

low, unintelligible voices. I looked round the cellar and saw, to my surprise, that there were many more people than I had at first thought crowding around a dark, damp, corner of the bar. There were at least twenty-five people standing around.

Damp!

I decided at last that this was not a very good place to find a story. So I got up, and walked to the door. As I stepped out the door, I realized that it was later than I had thought. It was dusk and full darkness was rapidly approaching. It was then that I felt a feeling of fear, of evil, and doom.

I wonder why you decided that? Your motivation to leave seems a bit weak, when you've described how ominous and mysterious it was. That ties back to 'we didn't know what we were looking for anyway' and it seems a bit weak.

The complete story was three times this length and I read and made comments on it all.

Next day, I brought the tape to school and gave it to David: he listened to it at home that night. A few days later I asked him for his reaction, and he said …

> It was interesting because I've never really heard one of my own stories. The only time I've heard it is if I've been reading one. It's good to hear it coming from someone else.
>
> You read it differently than me. Faster. I read it slower because I know how I expect it to go. But when someone's reading it from paper they don't really see that. The way you read it, things seemed to run into each other more. In future, I reckon I'd go closer over my story, expecially to look at commas, so you didn't go so fast.
>
> Also you said it was a bit weak, where he left the bar. I agree it did seem to fall a bit flat.
>
> Teachers usually talk about the whole story, not the parts of it. But this approach is good because you know which parts to work on.
>
> It's good that you weren't telling me how to improve it. That allows me to create my own story, instead of copying what the teacher tells me to do.

Now this is an articulate self-assessment grounded in the student's experience of hearing how his work was read.

It took me seven minutes to make David's tape; that is the time it took to read the whole piece and make the comments. Seven minutes is quite a long time to spend on one piece of writing, but many teachers spend longer than that reading and writing comments on a story of that length.

Here is how I have worded instructions for teachers who have used this approach.

Showing how you read

In this method of responding to students' writing you are encouraged to 'take it easy on yourself'.

It can be quite a strain to come up with a coherent perspective on a student's piece of writing. And then we have to work out how to express it to the student. And there are thirty of them! And probably 5 × 30!

In this approach you are asked only to share what you are thinking as you read the piece of writing. It is the writer's responsibility to form an overall impression of your reactons and to decide what to do as a result of your feedback.

Your **role** is that of reader, not teacher. Your task is to be **doing** the curriculum (in this case, reading), openly and with involvement; not **commenting** on the curriculum (that is, commenting on the student's writing). Teachers' comments are usually less direct, more abstract and more processed than the raw material of your reading which is asked for here.

Some guidelines

Read a little. Then record what you are thinking. 'Now I'm thinking …'. If you move into reading the piece dramatically to emphasize what you are making of it, with other thoughts interspersed, making a continuous record, that's fine.

Whichever way you do it, make sure you indicate on the tape where you're up to as you share your thoughts.

Five types of reaction that are useful to express are:
(1) Impact: 'Now this part seems very strong to me …' or 'I agree with this part'.
(2) Confusion/Mismatch:'Now I can't see how the latter part of this paragraph goes with the first part.'
(3) Overload: 'Now I'm finding it hard to keep all these different things in mind.'
(4) Underload: 'Now I'm thinking, why doesn't he get to the point.'
(5) Predictions: 'Now I'm thinking, it will be good if she gives me an example of this.'

If you find yourself making teacher-type comments on the writing ('This is good: you could have done so-and-so'), express them. If you try to hold onto them you'll freeze up! but don't let comments like these dominate. Try to keep the principal focus on your reading of the writing.

Can this seriously be suggested as being easier on the teacher than writing an overall comment? Yes. It is easier because it is more enjoyable than writing comments. (This way there is no writing at all.) I felt a sense of release — of just being able to talk, not having to struggle over the writing.

The longest tape I've made was nine minutes, and in that time I recorded a mass of specific reactions to a year 9 student's piece. The piece of work and my responses form Appendix 2 of this book.

As soon as the students had received a tape back about a piece of writing which they had offered for this purpose, we asked **them** to try to make a tape about a piece written by their writing partner. We gave them a one page instruction sheet which was similar to the instructions presented above.

The students made their cassette recordings at home. This meant they were familiar with the recording equipment. More importantly, they gave a response to a piece of writing when they were ready to do so — not because it had just been shoved in front of them: this increases the likelihood that they will give detailed responses. Making the recordings at home can also increase the toughness of their reaction because the comments are made remote from the writer, away from where the writer and reader normally interact: so the distance between writer and reader more closely approximates that which applies to most writing, whether it be for a teacher (who will often look at it out of class) or another audience.

The following three examples illustrate the range of responses in that year 9 class.

Year 9 students showing how they read: three examples

Some teachers have been fearful that this approach is dangerous. They think that students need to be protected, because they cannot cope with detailed reactions like these. In the light of these fears, I was very interested to hear a tape Emily made about a story by Janet, because Emily told me (after she made the tape), 'I didn't like it much at all. It was pretty weak all through.' On her tape, the most negative thing Emily said was:

At the end it says that Paula would pour a pot of hot coffee over the nurse, but I don't think anyone that's insane would really try out that idea.

and most of what she recorded was more like this:

"As she paced the floor of her cell", I like that bit. You can tell she is in gaol now, really desperate. She's like a caged cat trying to get out. (This is Emily's image, not Janet's) ... in a state of shock it says in the story. You put your sympathies immediately with her. There's a really good picture of guards poking fun at her. She's getting really desperate.

Because the instructions direct the reader to the particulars of the piece, global criticisms are not called for. Emily's overall evaluation of Janet's story is irrelevant. It is how she reads it that is important; and Janet used Emily's comments when she revised it into a much more polished story.

The least detailed reading was made by a boy who read a quite accomplished story, by Chris, which concerned 'a group of Soviet-backed terrorists who take over Elizabeth High School'. This reader read the story onto the tape adding only these comments.

I'm finding the story O.K.

So far I reckon it's good. I can hardly wait till the end.

Finding it a bit hard to read some of these words.

I'm wishing that you'd get on with the story, because so far I reckon it's pretty good, petty exciting.

In this case the boy had read the story aloud and seemed to have forgotten to make many comments. Even so the reading served as a confirmation and celebration of the writer's achievement. The writer, Chris, found the tape to be enjoyable and reinforcing …

He enjoyed it! He didn't pick up on spelling errors. The teachers think that we're talking on a lower basis than they are, so they won't give us too many extravagant words. They just say 'That's a very good story' and well, what else is there to say?

The third example is very detailed. Adam wrote a piece called 'Winter'. His writing partner, another Chris, spoke for eight minutes on the tape: only a selection of his comments appear here. Then follows Adam's revision after having heard Chris's comments. I have included quite a lot of this example for two reasons. Firstly, I am confident many teachers would be at a loss as to how to respond constructively to Adam's first draft (it is a good piece to use in workshops with teachers). Secondly, even though Chris's responses did not show an unusual insight or sophistication, Adam's revision, after hearing Chris's comments, demonstrated a marked improvement in that he took the reader into account so much more into the second version.

WINTER

Winter is, I think the longest season out. Your lucky enough even to see the sun. But when it does it's a relief. Winter is different in many countries, white Winters in most of the Northern Hemisphere and wet Winters in the Southern Hemisphere it also comes at different times. When it's Summer in the Northern, it's Winter in the Southern.

[Chris's response]

Adam, I've just finished reading your first paragraph of your story called 'Winter'. I'm feeling that you're a person who's expressing yourself quite freely. In your first sentence where it says 'Winter, is, I think…'. Now, I think that's a key points to this… 'the longest season out'. 'Season out.' the word 'out' and 'I think' are something that makes the reader, which is me, feel that you're very outgoing with it, which I think from pieces I've read is really good.

What do you mean by 'you're lucky enough to see the sun'? You haven't gone into saying what Winter really is, but then again, a bit further ahead, you've gone into describing what it's like in the northern hemisphere and the southern, whereas people really know that up in the northern it's just snowing and cold and down here it's just cold and wet, which I think is a bit too plain *and you've really hit an area where people already know that. There's not really much point in saying all that I don't think, but I'll see what I think of your second paragraph.*

We Australians think that it's cold outside in Winter but think about the Refugees, hundreds and thousands of them. Their lucky enough to even get an ounce of heat in Winter. Even sometimes there's not enough clothing to put on their backs. But we can name many things that keep us warm throughout the Winter, gas fires, coast, heaters …

I thought in your second paragraph you would have gone into describing, say, a place like the snowy mountains and … (He went on with a long commentary on the second paragraph).

People rely on Winter too as well. Farmers need the rain to irrigate the land. (Australia for example, if our crops didn't get rain, we would have to buy wheat, barley and other crops from other countries.) But too much rain is a disaster.

This is chipping and changing, although it's on the same subject. You … (He continued with a long reading of the third paragraph).

Winter can be a killer as well in the way of Floods, Cyclones and Tidalwaves. All the natural disasters make you wonder who is really in the head office up in the sky. Does He really want this race to build into the foundations He's already layed out by Him, or does He think He's made a miracle? Or is He trying to stop the population from over flowing the boundaries of the world? But if you've been in one of the terrifying incidents, maybe in their mysterious mind they may have the answer.

You've gone on to say in a completely new paragraph, 'Winter can be a killer as well in the way of floods, cyclones and tidal waves'. Now I don't see it as being directly involved with crops and going any further with refugees, although in some sense it does if they're refugees from cyclones, floods and things like that. I don't think they get cyclones up in the northern hemisphere, around Europe. You've gone on even further to describe them as natural disasters which they are.

And then you've gone on to speak about who's really in charge of the head office up in the sky. Now, I think it would have been better to say the word God, you know. That sort of says it all in one word, 'Who's in charge up there?' When you go on to say, 'Has He made a mistake? Or is He trying to keep the population under control by wiping a few of us off with floods', another way of putting it is, 'Is He trying to punish us or something?' (He said quite a lot more about the fourth paragraph).

When there's a break in the weather, I enjoy going outside and just watching the clouds move around in the sky by the strongly blowing wind. Sometimes I could stay outside for hours staring at the clouds. You can see many pictures in the clouds, lions, dogs. When you least expect it, strong winds pop up and wind through your body. Wind is a deadly part of Winter.

The End

by Adam Clavell

All the new paragraphs are really surprising me, because now you've gone into talking about how you get out and lie on the back lawn. I guess you'd lie on the back lawn and watch the clouds change shape with the wind. That to me doesn't quite seem right to go out up the back when it's cold and wet, although there's a break in the weather, it still seems ... it's still wet, although it's stopped raining. Rain is dripping off leaves. Water would be a better word. And, you know, who'd go out there and just look up at the clouds, when it's colder? You've gone from, ... violence, I guess would be the word, in cyclones and tidal waves and floods to watching peaceful shapes of lions and dogs changing in the sky, with the wind. And then you've gone on to say 'the wind is a deadly part of winter'. That should have been in your fourth paragraph, not in your fifth ... is the way I see it because, the fourth one is describing the dangers of it, and of what actually happens, whereas in the fifth, you're talking about peaceful things, I guess. But then you can't really pick up weak points and clump around parts that should be elsewhere because there's more just written of how you feel about it in a sort of diary. I would have thought that maybe you just jotted these thoughts down. How you felt about it and just put them together in a story because the way I see it is about how you feel about winter and how you see things.'

Adam's revision of 'WINTER'

This story is about what I have heard, read, thought about and my feelings on Winter.

Winter is, I think the longest season of all four. The sun is a rare sight, but when you do see it, it's a relief. Winter is different in many countries, from wet winters in the Southern Hemisphere to white winters in the Northern, but the cold is a part of all types of winters.

We Australians think that it's cold outside but think of all those homeless refugees hundreds of thousands of them. Not enough money to get any warm clothes (such as jumpers). I don't know if I could stand that, wondering how I am going to keep warm throughout Winter, but I suppose you'd have to wouldn't you? But I could name endless things that are everyday things to us that keep us warm; fires, coats, heaters …

People rely on winter as well. Farmers in particular need the rain to irrigate the land. If there isn't enough the whole country would have to seek help from neighbouring countries for their cereal crops. But too much is a disaster.

Winter is a killer (destroyer) in the way of Floods, Cyclones, Tidalwaves. All these and other natural disasters that have occurred makes you wonder what He really expects of us. Does He want to literally destroy the human population with all these disasters or just control the population. Flash Floods is one of the worst — one minute it is just spitting and then in the next minute rivers overflow and the country is in panic. But winter isn't always this way.

When there is no rain or snow the wind, a deadly part of Winter, will probably be blowing. A cyclone will take your roof of your and even your whole house, lift it into the sky and drop it somewhere else but the average wind wouldn't do that much damage. If you go outside to play when there is no rain about the wind will find a way to get through your coat and wind its way through your body, but wind also does things that we like to happen such as moving a windmill to pump up water from the underground boar.

Chris's comments are detailed and they are tough on Adam, because they present him with the meeting between what he wrote and a reader's experience. There is so much more here than 'It's interesting' or 'It's good' or 'I can't understand it', which are common responses when students are asked to comment on a piece of writing as a whole.

It is important to emphasize that Chris received no lengthy training before making this response. He demonstrated that this detailed responsiveness was available, simply waiting to be tapped.

We can see that Adam kept many of Chris's reactions in mind when he redrafted 'Winter'. How did he feel about the tape Chris made?

Adam: It was good because I see how other people understood my writing. Teachers might say 'The beginning wasn't good, you could probably work on that a bit more'. But most of the time they say 'Overall it's a good story', they don't say what your weak points and your good points are.

When you listen to it you feel a bit low, but after you finish listening to it, you just understand it. You're not feeling low anymore.

Brian: I think many teachers are a bit too scared to say 'that's a bit weak', so maybe they suggest how it could have been. What do you think? Is it a good idea for you to hear other kids saying where they think it is weak?

Adam: I don't think it'd discourage you, if you knew they're taking it seriously. Then you know you've got some improvement to do in your writing.

How did Chris feel about making the tape?

Chris: The instructions were clear but hard to do. When you read the instructions, you think 'Well that's easy'. But when you go to do it, it's really hard.

I just said what I thought about it. I didn't think he'd be angry at me for bashing his writing ... going through and thinking, no, I don't like this, I don't like that and contradicting it. I get on well with Adam, so I didn't think he would hate me for it.

IMPLEMENTING 'SHOWING HOW YOU READ' IN THE CLASSROOM

The students read each other's pieces in quite different ways. I felt there was no need to bring them back rigidly to the instructions. I think the main benefit of the procedure is that student writers see their work treated **seriously**, even savoured, by their readers.

Adam warned that students should have some choice in who they get such a response from:

If someone is mucking around while he's doing it, well then you don't take it real seriously. It's best if you have one of your friends do it, not one of your worst enemies.

Using cassettes allows the teacher to monitor how seriously students are tackling the task: it can be treated as an assignment for oral language and reading. As students develop a level of proficiency in giving their reactions this way, and as the writers learn what to expect, it is not necessary to continue to use cassettes, unless the writer wants it.

Volunteers, parents and student readers from other year levels can also be taught to show how they read students' work on cassette. Exposing students to the different types of reactions they receive to one piece of writing is an important part of the education of a writer. Some readers are more sensitive, more ready to accept; others are more judgemental. But both have something to tell the writer.

Do the student writers take up the challenge to digest all the specific reactions into an overall perspective? In a sense the answer to that is 'no'. They take some comments to heart and ignore others. Sometimes they redraft, sometimes not. But I think they generally learn someting from the comments and **they** decide which — we do not have to find things we could comment on and then select from them. The writer does the selecting.

Some teachers have suggested that the instructions include that the piece be read once through so that the reader gets a picture of it as a whole, before the reactions are recorded. This would increase the time spent on each piece by a few minutes. I know some students do this, but I suggest to them that they not do so. My impression is that the immediacy of one's reactions is muted if one spends some of the time trying to remember first reactions. The commenting becomes more processed, more like work, and less comments are recorded. If I were moved to reread a piece that would itself be part of my reaction. But often writing has to rely on its first impact and that is what is recorded on tapes I make.

A STUDENT READS HIS OWN WORK

One of the goals of this procedure is that, by making cassettes, students will strenghten the 'other self', the reader of their writing.
They can demonstrate their ability to be readers of their own writing by making tapes about pieces they have produced. As an example, here is the first paragraph of a story and the beginning section of a tape a year 9 writer made of his reading of his own work.

Draft

An ear splitting scream arose from the courtyard, as a bayonet pierced a human body. Slowly, slowly, very very slowly, a man began to descend the badly rotten stairs. The hungry, diseased prisoners watched the elderly man from their bamboo cage in the southwestern corner of the yard. 'The bastard's taking his time,' said Johnson. 'Yeah, does it everytime' agreed Sergeant Downs. The man stopped at the bottom of the stairs perspiration glistening on his bald head. His old wrinkled hand opened a breast-pocket on his kakhi uniform, from which a packet of cigarettes were removed. With the same hand he replaced the packet and lit the native tobacco. Stained teeth appeared as a smile flicked across his face at the sight of the burning tobacco.

Chris Northeast

Chris on his own draft

In the beginning, it's got 'An ear splitting scream arose from the courtyard'. That, I think, is, how can I put it? … Sort of shocks the reader at first, it sort of catches his eye. Then it goes on, 'as a bayonet pierced a human body'. That for some would sound pretty gory. But then it goes on 'Slowly, slowly, very very slowly, a man began to descend the badly rotten stairs'. I think the slowly part might be over-emphasized a bit much. But the badly rotten stairs seemed to fit in with the courtyard. And then it goes into 'hungry, diseased prisoners'. That gives you a good description of what they are and what they're in, 'bamboo cage'. Then it's got a bit of swearing which, I guess, for prisoners in a cage would be quite natural.

Then my story goes on about the man descending the stairs and when he gets to the bottom, and the perspiration and it goes on describing his uniform, his khaki and then it goes on to how he's taking his time. That I feel, as the reader, is starting to get a bit boring and monotonous. It's suddenly slowed down to this man's pace, which for me seems terribly slow.

I'm getting a feeling as if I'm actually there, actually in the courtyard.

How would we use Chris's response to his piece? It guides us to comment on the aspects of his piece that he seems most unsure about. A few days after he made that tape, I got Chris to listen to it and write down a sentence or two summarizing what he was thinking about the writing 'at the moment, as the writer of the piece'. I was asking him to have a dialogue between writer and reader roles.

He wrote: 'The story is descriptive, but because of the detail it (the story) doesn't move along at a quick exciting pace.' I read that and, asked.

Brian: That slowly, slowly bit. Have you come to a decision about that?

Chris: I haven't come to a decision, because an old guy, who's obviously of some rank and authority doesn't rush around. He takes his time. He knows he's got time. He makes time for himself. But that reflects into the story. You can't suddenly rush. You've got to take your time at his pace, but in doing that you don't get an exciting story. I'm trying to get him to the guy who's been pierced with the bayonet. But I get furstrated because of his pace. I can't get there that quickly.

Brian: When you said slowly, slowly, I reckon *that* was overdone, because all the rest of the paragarph does it for you. You're slowing us down just as

you've said. You don't need to be so obvious by saying slowly, slowly —
we get that message when you make us slow down — which is more
powerful, so if it were mine, I'd take slowly, slowly out, but I would
hate to think you're going to think, 'I'd better leave it all out'.

Chris's evaluation of 'Showing how you read' was:

I think it's good ripping it to shreds sort of thing because it brings out
more for future writing. I can see where I've blundered up on it. Things
that haven't come over as strong as they should be … that were too weak.
    If at the beginning of the year you started that, by the end of the year,
you'd know how different people had taken your pieces of writing. If
you're trying to write a real sad piece and someone doesn't see it that way,
you can learn to express yourself in the writing so that they get exactly
what you mean.

The main advantage of 'showing how you read', is that students and
teachers can say so much about a piece of writing when they respond, as
readers, to the particulars of the writing, rather than trying to make more
highly processed general comments. It can be introduced slowly,
practised with volunteers, and not forced onto students unless they
choose the piece of writing and the reader.
    This approach is not meant to completely replace more thought-out,
processed comments on writing. They have their place and it is
important to teach students the appropriate vocabulary for such
comments. This will be best done after they have experienced more
detailed reactions like those presented in this section.

MORE PROCESSED READER REACTIONS

Detailed responses like those discussed in the previous section cannot
be the regular focus of class discussion, group work or talking with
individual students in class. They take too long.
    Are there ways of talking about writing **which** are more succinct yet
have the advantage of the method just described, that they rely
principally on reader response rather than commenting **upon** writing?
    Reader response is a better starting point than commenting, because
students simply **do not** learn to link paragraphs better, write stronger
conclusions or eradicate run-on sentences by our telling them that they
need to do those things. The perception of a need to change must be
part of their experience, not just ours. This means that if students are to
develop their writing, they must be able to read their work and see the
need for the changes themselves. Our principal role is to show them how

we and others read their work, and to teach them different ways of reading it themselves, so that they can develop as writers.

Here is an approach which I have used. It is not as powerful as the more detailed, raw reactions of the previous section but it provides a practical and effective way of thinking about and responding to writing in the often noisy atmosphere of the classroom.

There are three questions which I ask of a piece of writing.

(1) What do I find as the key idea or centre of gravity of the piece?

(2) Can I see a pattern in the writing which indicates how the elements in the piece relate to each other?

(3) Did the writer lead me to appreciate the centre and how the elements in the piece relate to each other?

Firstly, '**What do I find as the key idea or centre of gravity of the piece?**' The term centre of gravity, which I usually abbreviate to centre, comes from Peter Elbow's *Writing without teachers*,[2] and I find it useful to create a special piece of jargon to highlight that I expect students to think and talk about their writing in a specific way.

This first question is important because a reader wants to remember something of what the writing was doing for him or her. It confronts the fundamental question, 'What is the point?'. For the writing to have impact the centre must carry information and be focused. 'Seals' would not constitute a centre, whereas 'Seals should be protected' would.

Because I can't get to talk individually with each student very often, I teach the students to find centres in what we read and listen to, material from our class and from outdise it. And often writers are asked to describe the centres they find in their own writing. Centres can be expressed in the writer's words or in those of the reader. Sometimes we focus on what is remembered from a piece several days after it has been read.

Finding a centre is a fascinating task. Everyone who responds is correct in that they find and report back their experience of the writing. Poor readers and listeners give feedback which is important to the writer, for they tell what confusions arise in some readers' minds. At the same time, it remains a challenging task, for sometimes a reader will encapsulate a piece so elegantly that his response touches others. Sometimes the writer jots down that way of expressing it.

Often I encourage the student to strengthen a centre rather than leave it weak or vague. This was illustrated when I talked to Craig, a year 9 boy at Ingle Farm High School, after reading the first draft of his piece 'The farmer's choice'.

The farmer's choice

Everyone would expect a farm to have lots of livestock such as chooks, ducks etc. Lush green or brown paddocks, stacks of hay neatly formed, sheds with tools arranged on walls or in boxes. Pipes, metal, wood, paint tins and spare parts, hung on the wall or planted in the corner tidily. You'll see his vehicles parked in a shed or under some sort of cover and maybe ploughs, hay stackers and farm machinery.

This would be a sterotype of a farm but I know a ripper of change.

This farm I know has only 4 horses, two dogs and chickens. Large paddocks have rarely been ploughed but change colours as the seasons go by. The tractor and pick up truck are left out in the weather to rust. Car bodies are strewn over an area with the broken promise that they will soon be put together and in running order.

The shed is so unorganized with tools lying everywhere, paint cans, wood, car and bike parts, containers, wire, gallon drums, machinery and all of this is caked in dust straw mud and chook dung and feathers. The Moto go-carts seat filled with straw is a great nest. The house needs a paint both in and outside. Kids' toys are lying everywhere and the carpets are badly grimed with mud and dust.

There are some features though that make the place a resort. For instance a lot of land for us to ride mini bikes with jumps and trees to form a track, a large dug in swimming pool, colourful trampoline (olympic size) and gym equipment layout on the farm is excellent but it does need a lot of work. But I guess its the farmer's choice.

Brian: That's strong, the contrast between the normal farm and the one you want to describe. But I'm not quite sure why it's important. I don't understand what the centre of the piece is. What is it?

Craig: The second type of farm.

Brian: That's a bit vague. What are you telling the reader about the second type of farm?

Craig: Just, what kind of farm I know.

Brian: Yeah, but what's important about it, that makes you write about it?

Craig: How much different is it from people's thoughts of a farm, its appearance, the attitude of the farmer, his way of working.

Brian: O.K. It's different. Anything else? Anything stronger than just that its different?

Craig: Even though I explained the farm being like this, not looking like a proper farm, there's still a lot of good things about it.

Next day, Craig explained he'd rewritten 'The farmer's choice' to emphasize the centre more.

Craig's second draft 'The farmer's choice'

Everyone would expect a farm to have large heards of livestock, sheep, cows, horses, chickens and ducks etc. These kinds of animals being the money earning objects of the farm. Lush green or brown paddocks, stacks of hay neatly formed, sheds with tools arranged on walls or in boxes. Pipes, metal, wood, paint tins and spare parts, hung on the tin walls or planted in the corner tidily. You'll see his vehicles parked in a shed or under some sort of cover and maybe ploughs, hay stackers and other pieces of farm machinery.

The farmers work is endless. You would be sure to see him up early in the morning to milk the cows, start the tractor to plough, fix something in the shed or tend to the animals. He will work until light allows or until his desired time. He is interested in sport but has no time to be involved.

This would be the stereotype of a farmer and his farm but I know a great deal of a change in the normal view of a farm.

This farm I know has only four horses, two dogs and chickens. The large paddocks have rarely been ploughed but change colours as the seasons go by. The tractor and pick up truck are left out in the weather to rust. Car bodies are strewn over a large area with the broken promise that they will soon be put together and in running order. The shed is so unorganized with tools lying everywhere, paint cans, wood, car and bike parts, containers, wire, gallon drums, machinery and all of this is caked in dust, straw, mud, chicken dung and feathers. The Motorized Go-Cart seat filled with straw makes a great nest for chickens. The house needs a good rub down and paint. Kids toys lie everywhere on the badly mud and dust grimed carpets.

The layout of the farm gives you the impression that the house was dumped in one spot and everything formed around it since — the shed, fences, trees, paddocks and driveway. The farmer there has his own business. He coaches and plays basketball, tennis, gymnastics and competitive horseriding. The farm, I don't think, is really serious. Just possibly a hobby or a side interest away from normal urban life or just somewhere to own and ride horses and bikes etc.

There are some features though that make the place a resort. For instance, a lot of land for us to ride mini bikes, with jumps and trees to form a track. A large dug in swimming pool, a colourful olympic size trampoline and gym equipment. The farm is a great set up and is excellent fun for us kids but it does need a lot more work done to it.

But I guess it's the farmers choice!

If I am responding to a student individually and I find it hard to find a clear centre, I'll ask the writer what he or she sees and I don't expect that all their writing should have clear centres, for these are first drafts.

It is only this, the first of the three questions, that I have succeeded in getting students to use. It is a simple approach, which is why it it valuable. It opens up discussion in a straightforward, uncomplicated way. From the centre, it is possible to question for elaboration. 'Seals should be protected? By whom? ... Where? ... How? ...'

When a centre has been found, I am ready to consider the second question, '**Can I see a pattern in the writing which indicates how the elements in the piece relate to each other?**' I often find myself drawing a little diagram to indicate which elements are related and which are not, as happened when I talked to Craig about 'The man in the iron mask'.

The man in the iron mask
By Craig Feckner

He is alone
In a barren room.
No furniture or luxury, just solid brick walls.
A single stair case leading out from his dungeon.
There is no hope for escape for he is chained to the
wall like a ferocious untame animal.
He is cold in the chamber.
Only a single barred window breaks the gloom and darkness
And a piercing ray of sunlight helps keep his body from freezing,
His clothes are old and torn.
He can only hear the outside world in the distance.
For no person goes near the forbidden walls.
And no birds nest in the cracks on the outside wall or
In between the roof shingles.
His mask gets dark and cold.
And condensation and an umbearable heat surrounds his
head when he breathes heavily.
And the carbon dioxide cannot escape through the small
breathing hole.
His mask does not cover a scarred, wounded, war torn face.
But just his manly features from the recognition of others.
He only thinks of the past, for he feels there is no future
Just eat and drink and sleep.
But he does not know that he mob will storm the
Bastille.
And he will be free.

Brian: The line about dwelling on the past because he feels there is no future. That's insightful. Let's look at the structure of the thing. What are the main elements?

Craig: The dungeon, the mask and … that he'll be set free.

Brian: O.K., well you've got a strong contrast between the dungeon and freedom, so that links those two. The last line about freedom is very strong because of the strength of your description of the dungeon. What are the links between the dungeon and the mask?

Craig: Because the mask is important, I thought about bringing it in earlier. But then I decided not to. Because the dungeon and the mask are kind of the same.

Brian: Yeah, what about freedom and the mask. I don't see much link between them. I'm left wondering whether he'd wear the mask when he's free.

Craig: No, I don't think so.

Brian: Maybe you could do another piece that explores that.

Craig: A sequel.

The scribbled diagram looked like this:

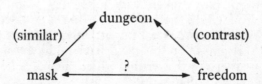

If I find a pattern in the writing which connects the different elements in a satisfying way, then I consider the third question, 'Did the writer lead me to appreciate the centre and how the elements in the piece relate to each other?' Various aspects of the writer's style and arrangement of information can be considered here. In practice I usually focus only on the beginning of the piece and have the students consider 'Did it begin in such a way that I wanted to read further?' I stress here that as well as being clear, bold and structured, effective writing attracts the reader's interest.

And that is the three-step approach to first drafts. Discussions might focus on all three questions (usually when the centre is clear and bold and the writing structured) or only the first (if the centre is not clear).

To finish this section, I discuss two students' pieces; in each, according to my reading, the writer presents a clear centre and in a controlled way leades us to appreciate how the elements of the piece interrelate. The first piece is by Deb (year 9) and is called 'Allen'.

On a Thursday night of the schools variety show I met a nice guy named Allen. I was just walking in the main door and a boy said 'hi' I said hallo and went to get changed after our act I went and stood at the back of the room so I could see the rest of the show. Allen was sitting next to me and people kept on coming into the room and I could not see the show. When franks esposito's band came on I ask Allen if I could use half of his chair with him to stand on after we started to talk. He asked for my phone number I told him we have just got the phone number and I don't know it. He asked me if I wonted a lift home but I said no again. Well on friday Allen came around my house and asked me if I was going to the variety show tonight I said yes and he said he will pick me up in about half an hour I got ready as fast as I could. Well in the car I made him promise that he would not come around again he also made me promise that I will phone him up. Well Allen comes and see me at school every day now and I like him a lot. He has not asked me to go around with him yet. But I hope he asks me soon. The thing I can't tell mum is that Allen is 21 years old.

What do I find as the centre? I chose the last sentence. Most in the class chose 'he has not asked me to go around with him yet'. We discussed these two. The last sentence struck me because it clarified the relationships between the three characters (Deb, Allen, Mum). I think the students were more taken with being left wondering about the future. Deb listened to her writing being discussed sensibly and energetically by involved readers. Importantly we were not getting into a discussion of her values. To this day I have no idea if it is a true story.

Can I see a pattern in the writing which indicates how the elements relate together? Yes. The writing clearly describes Allen's growing importance to Deb (caution, attraction, hoping). It becomes more significant by incorporating Mum and indicating how she affects Deb and Allen's relationship.

Have I been led to appreciate the centre and the relatedness? Yes. I enjoyed the gradual, detailed build-up of the friendship and the tension of 'I made him promise ...' which together developed a clear context for appreciating the openness of Deb's description of her relationship with Allen (the second to last sentence) and the shock of her dilemma in relating to Allen and Mum. Because I saw it as a very strong piece of writing, I was keen to see it polished and we went on to talk about that.

Notice that the responses to the questions are personal, and that articulate readers will differ in their answers. Furthermore, answers to the three questions overlap. I do not see any problem with that. The value, as I see it, is that the students and I consider the work seriously as readers.

The second piece is by Rachel (year 2) and is untitled.

> One day I was crying and my dad said what is the mater mum wont let me have horse I will be you one said dad. Thank yuo and I lived happey ervy after.

What do I find as the centre? Rachel wants a horse. Can I see a pattern which indicates how the elements relate? Yes, she clearly indicates how important the idea of having a horse is to her, and she indicates how her mum and dad relate to that. Have I been led to appreciate the centre and the relatedness? Yes, with an arresting beginning. It would be easier to appreciate with a couple more full stops and I would look at that, as she has used two correctly.

This approach, relying on looking for a centre and relatedness can be applied to any type of writing. Bernard Newsome has described a similar way of looking at the structure of students' narratives.

STUDENTS' NARRATIVES

Newsome[3] has drawn on the work of Labov[4] to describe students' narrative writing. He suggests that a narrative often involves 'The following kind of organization:

Phase 1:   The scene is set for the events to occur.
Phase 2:   A sequence of events is presented, out of which the critical event(s) emerges.
Phase 3:   The critical event(s) is presented and focused.
Phase 4:   The critical event(s) and its aftermath is evaluated.

This fourth phase involves the writer reflecting on what the critical event meant to her.

Phase 4 is critical because 'the point of narrative is to evaluate, so writer and reader must be left with a focus on the significance of events rather than on the fact of their happening. Failure to achieve this leaves both writer and reader with a bare and pointless narrative'.

So in responding to students' narratives we can look for the critical event (centre) and to the writer's evaluations of that critical event, whether they be presented explicitly, which might be more common in personal narrative or more subtly (perhaps more common in a story). This can be looked at by diagramming elements in the story, and the writer's apparent relationship to them.

Newsome quotes 'My Ride', by a 12-year-old girl, as an example.

My ride

One morning I got up and walked out to get my horse. I walked down the lane and into the larger paddock. After a while Debbie, Amanda and Lisa came and they all went down and got their horses. Debbie and Lisa said to Amanda and I 'Would you like to go for a ride down the lane', Amanda and I agreed. After a while down the lane we decided to go to Debbie's place.

We rode along the railway and then across the 'Main Street of Mornington'. We then went to the place where the new 'Safeway' was being built.

We then, after a while arrived at Debbie's house. The other girls and I let our horses go and had some lunch.

After about two hours we went down and mounted up. Then we started to ride back.

It was starting to get cloudy when we rode along the railway. We then came to the Collage were we all rode throw.

By then Debbie and I swapt horses and we were ridding again. After we got inside the grounds Rocky reard up and fell on Debbie. Rocky got up and took off for home, luckily enough that was not far. Debbie laid there for awhile more fritened than anything. She was alright and so was Rocky.

The critical event is the rearing of the horse and its falling on the rider, and its aftermath, their mutual recovery. But what did the rearing, the falling and the recovery mean to the writer? Has she indicated their significance by indicating connections between those elements and herself? the answer is 'not clearly'.

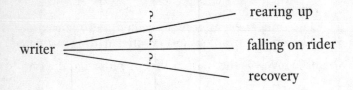

The teacher's strategy can be to ask the writer to help the reader more by indicating what these elements meant to her, and by extension what they are likely to mean to the reader.

ARTICULATE READER OR JUDGE?

When I disucss centres and relatedness, I am trying to describe articulately my reading of the student's work ('This is what I'm making of it'), rather than making judgements of it ('This is bad because those things don't relate together'). I emphasize to students that first drafts need not have clear centres nor relatedness, that we write such drafts in order to start finding these structural qualities.

I suppose that students sometimes take my reactions as overly judgemental. So it is important to get **them** to reflect on their work in this way. When they do I quite often see how insensitive my reading has been. I'm often educated to see much more in their work than what I pick up on a hasty first reading.

By **dwelling** on the reading of the student's work, the teacher earns the right to **then** praise, criticize and suggest improvements,

Similarly, if a strong pattern is established in the class so that the students **dwell on** discovering what is in their own and each others' writing, **then** the teacher can move on to help them look at how their writing might be improved. Strategies for doing this are presented in the next chapter.

6 Helping Students Identify Strengths in Their Writing and Goals for Impovement

In the previous chapter, I argued that comments on students' writing are only useful if they influence the way the students read their own writing.

Have the more usual teacher-type comments a role to play — comments which describe what a student has achieved and which attempt to diagnose what the student needs to learn?

Such comments will have very little effect if the student does not re-read the piece of writing with them in mind. Further, they will be of little consequence if the student is not going to write similar pieces in the near future.

However, there are three situations in which teachers' instructional comments can be effective.

Firstly, if the student is going to revise a piece and can see a problem but not the solution, the teacher can suggest things to be considered. The more involved we are as readers of the writing first, the more we earn the right to make suggestions as to how problems might be avoided, when our intuition and observation of the student suggest that the comments will be heard.

Secondly, in classrooms where students are used to consciously experimenting in writing, the teacher can suggest that they try specific changes in their writing and then read it through and assess themselves whether the changes work.

Thirdly, because teacher comments are often expressed in more general terms than reader responses, they are useful for describing patterns in a student's work. Once a pattern is isolated, closer attention can be given to helping the student read to identify the strength or weakness.

It is important that there is continuity in the class work, so that assessment comments are seen to relate to future work. So often in English, this sense of continuity is lacking. There are students in most classes who have **never** got into the habit of considering the teacher's comments when next they write. For them, the comments are only justifications of the mark or grade given to that particular piece of work. Having read the comments for that purpose they are done with them.

Teachers can counteract this tendency by relating their comments to specific pieces of work which will be started in the next few days. ('Here are two things you could work on. Here are two things that stand you in good stead.') This requires that the programme lingers over particular genres or topics, or sequences them in a developmental progression, rather than flitting from one type of writing to another.

DEVELOPING CONTINUITY IN COMMENTS

Here is a system for providing a sense of continuity. The example comes from Janet Rowe's year 11 and 12 classes at Elizabeth High School. The focus is writing about literature. Janet explained:

As an English teacher at Year 12, I spend between twenty and forty minutes marking an essay. That seems a lot, but I've found I'm not unusual in this respect. Sometimes it takes a long time to figure out what they're talking about. Quite often you have to read an essay three times before you feel you can make a valid comment on it.

So you might spend eight hours or more marking Year 12 essays! We were wondering how much red marks, crossings out, rephrasings and a comment at the end actually taught kids. They didn't seem to relate comments from one piece of writing to the next — they had no sense of continuity or development.

Last year we decided to get a system going. Lola Brown helped me. I am still using it this year and will use it more widely next year.

I get the kids to keep all their essays in a folder. Stapled to the back of the folder is a sheet divided into two columns, one titled 'can do' and one 'need to learn' (see the example on pp. 78–79). Rather than write comments on their individual essays and then forget them, I put them on this sheet, so that they can be reminded of them each time. So, as the year goes on all the comments are assembled in one place.

In the 'can do' column the students get positive comments. In the 'need to learn' column, they get actual strategies they can use to improve their work. I try to limit it to two or three 'need-to-learns' at a time, so that they don't get swamped.

Need to Learn	Can do
① Introduction writing - too much jumbled together. Write introduction, then essay, go back and re-write intro. ② (a) "Making the play seem more realistic" had no subject or verb. (b) Two sentences written as one, joined by a comma. Write out sentences. Either make into 2 sentences or use joining word.	Shows real familiarity with the play. You are obviously selecting from a very great store of information. You write with vitality - your 'personal voice' comes through. Connect ideas of each paragraph.
Expression errors when you talk about poet's technique. You don't show that you understand the poems. Write out what Hangman, Good Sport, Good Friday mean in your own words. Then, in your own words write out how D. expresses himself in each. Then show the work to me.	Much better sentence construction.
① Colon to introduce quotes. ② Learn the spellings of words marked out.	Shows a much better grasp of the meaning of the poetry. More technically accurate sentences.
Read pge. 2 - it's disjointed. You make a point in each sentence without making clear the links between them. Maybe this is because it's nearly all generalizations - it needs some specific illustrations. ① You fail, usually, to refer to text to prove your point - it's not just on pge 2. that this occurs. Some careless sp. errors show a need to improve your proof reading skills.	Good clear introduction !! The essay gathers momentum and I love the way it develops up to the last point, showing terrific understanding of the essence of the book. Tremendous improvement in sentence construction and use of words.

Need to Learn	Can do
subject/verb. agreement Sentence construction faulty - rewrite.	

You need to learn to spell.
  tragic   oppressed
  dolent   loses
See me to explain use of
apostrophes.
Some non-sentences at ①
or clumsiness.
<u>Re-write them</u>
	Excellent use of language.
	Good use of examples to prove
	general statements.
	Good involvement in the
	novel.
	(You've come a long way baby!)

① You've lost control of the sen-
tences here.
  1(a) Here it reads as though the
wives have come home from the
pub.
    Re-write 1(a) & 1(b)
	Nice conclusion. Generally
	fluent but do keep an eye on
	that sentence construction.
	You show a good understanding
	of the texts.

SPELLING: Romanticism possessing portraying dispossessed oppression You can't 'conform' someone. Someone can be made to conform You could make clearer <u>connections</u> between the texts.	Really fantastic! Such an improve- ment in sentence construction! So articulate! You show a real familiarity with the books & a deep understanding of the issues raised by them. Excellent introduction — has every- thing, including the personal voice which shows confidence.
	Excellent use of reference to the text to prove your points.
Spelling (learn) tormented marriage breeder comparing futility ghost arouse ① Clumsy - rewrite ② Semi-colon not necessary. No clear development of essay - either <u>chronological sequence</u> of <u>events</u> or <u>topics</u> — <u>see me</u>	① Final paragraph very succinct.

At first glance this system seems fairly mechanistic. It seems to imply that the strengths observed are skills which can be trotted out at any time. We know that writing isn't like that. For example, to write a dramatic beginning is not to demonstrate a fixed skill of producing dramatic openings. But strengths can often refer to **understandings** that the student has. If the student has reworked a piece to make the beginning more dramatic, then the experience and understanding that he or she can do this can be listed as a strength, a resource which the teacher can refer to in discussing later pieces. So, while strengths and goals might sometimes be easily labelled skills like apostrophes or direct speech, they can also be **understandings** that the student can operate from in shaping work for an audience.

Janet continued by discussing the sorts of goal she identifies in the first column:

> I look for patterns, particularly in paragraphing, flow of ideas, sentence structure and punctuation: the more obvious things which they can improve on.
>
> There are some kids who have the same fault time and again, but at least with this system, they are aware of their errors; much more so than if you just mark them out every time. I think most kids don't get anything out of it when you mark out something and re-express it for them. I just write 'Still doing this'. When they're not improving, all you can do is go through it with them individually and hope. You can't do any more than that.
>
> If they're showing a continued improvement I'll write 'Once again you're continuing to …', to keep it in their minds.
>
> I've continued to use the system because, last year, I could see that those who used it did improve. They said it was really fantastic. When they looked back at the esays written early in the year, they saw so much improvement! And these were kids I'd taught the year before, when I hadn't noticed marked improvement.
>
> The improvement is right there, recorded on the sheet. It's something they can keep track of.
>
> Some kids have a tendency not to use the folders. So you have to say 'I will not give you a detailed comment if you don't hand it up in your folder'.
>
> That teaches them to do it. About ninety percent used the folders consistently last year. This year they're used by everyone, but some don't use them every time, if they're late with their work.
>
> I thought that this scheme might cut down the time I spent, but it hasn't. It takes the same time, but I feel my time is more usefully spent. They're getting something out of my twenty minutes or so.
>
> At report writing time, the scheme quickly gives me a much clearer idea of what they're doing. I open up each folder as I go to write the report, whereas I would never have gone through all their pieces of work to see all my comments.

Those of Janet's students whom I talked to were very positive about the system. For example:

> With this system, I'm improving. I can see it. It's more constant when the comments are together and you're faced with them. When you look back through the comments you think 'Well I've done that bit and I can see how I've improved my punctuation'. And so you go through, you think 'After I've written this one I'm going to go over it to see if I've got my tenses right'.

> The 'can do' comments are good because that boosts your ego a bit. I get more of them than the bad comments. I've concentrated on writing better introductions. I used to write just the same thing for the introduction and the conclusion.

Both these students used the assembled comments to help them articulate what they could do. The second student's reference to 'bad comments' made me suspect that he saw the 'need to learn' comments more as justifications of the mark, than as guides to development. He later confirmed that suspicion:

> When I get a mark, I look at the comments for that essay to see why I got that mark. I've never sat down and looked at all the comment at once. I should look at them more. I suppose I think I don't need the help, as I get quite good marks.

Other students had clearly drawn on Janet's suggestions for guidance:

> At home I've read through all the comments a few times, both just before writing an essay — and also just because it's interesting.

I asked Janet and the students if they had criticisms of the scheme.

> Janet: I haven't found a better method. The only regret is that it can be more obvious if they're not developing and they just can't seem to get past a block.

Most students had no criticisms of the system and thought it should have been introduced earlier in their schooling. However, one referred to the level of student involvement:

> It's just between Miss Rowe and the student. It might benefit others in the class if we could talk about it. If someone had a lot of run-on sentences, they could ask other kids how they learnt about that.

Actually, Janet had tried to involve the students' peers in the system. She had got them to write on the front of their folders, 'Choose a person to read your essays to in the light of previous comments, to suggest whether you have improved in the areas mentioned in the 'need to learn' column and whether you have maintained the skills mentioned in the 'can do' column'.

Janet: I don't think anyone's done that. They weren't committed
        enough to do it. Although I think it would have been valuable,
        you can't chase up things like that. If they're not prepared to do it,
        then they're not.

Two students commented ...

> I've never got someone to read it. They're too busy. I haven't
> thought about that since I wrote it down.

> I've had other kids read my work, but I can't see the need for
> them to check up on things listed on the sheet. I know what they
> are anyway.

There was another instruction which had also been largely ignored.
This was: 'On the front inside of the folder, write out my comment in
your own words.' There was no audience for this and the students saw
little point in it:

> I always understood what she wrote. She gave lots of examples. I can't see
> the point in writing it out if you understand it fully; and if you didn't,
> you'd go and ask her anyway.

Nevertheless, as a system for assembling teacher comments, this
approach seems to have worked well. Students who were motivated to
reflect on and improve their work went over all the teacher's comments
from time to time.

This method can be used when the teacher is also the judge of the
student's work, as Janet was. When that is so, students will be pressured
to take notice of the suggestions so as to satisfy the judge (and their
ownership of the writing will be somewhat diminished) but when the
students accept this apprenticeship-like situation, they can receive
useful help.

A second problem with operating this scheme as a teacher-judge is
that students who receive marks which satisfy them will often not be
highly motivated to consider the comments as guides to future writing.
The boy quoted earlier provided an example of that. This is an
inevitable problem when favourable judgements are expressed in
culturally powerful language like 'A' or '19/20' or 'excellent'. These
terms so powerfully connote emotional approval that they distract the
student from focusing on what has actually been achieved in the writing
itself.

Could a scheme like Janet's be implemented in place of grades or
marks? And could the students be more involved in discussing and
setting their own goals?

TEACHER–STUDENT NEGOTIATION OF GOALS FOR WRITING

Sr. Margaret Cain and I tried to set up a system based on Janet Rowe's, which involved talking to the students individually about goals for their writing.

We were working with two year 11 classes at Cabra Dominican College. One class had twenty students and one, thirty-two. Our plan was that I would help get the scheme going by team teaching with Sr. Margaret in first term. When it was established I would gradually withdraw and see how it operated with Margaret running it on her own. Here is how I described the system, before we started.[1]

I'll tell the student that in about a week's time, I want two pieces of work given to me for an intensive assessment (I'll record a date for each individual student).

The purpose of this assessment is to begin preparing a descriptiion of what the student can do in writing and a goal which the student can have for the future. I'll tell the student this is what it is for and ask him or her to write underneath their selected pieces what they see is being handled adequately in them. I'll give them a copy of criteria (Table 1) and they can just tick the appropriate ones if they want to, althought I'll ask them to describe other aspects as well.

I'll also ask them to indicate any aspects of their writing which they think should be improved. Lastly, I'll ask them to make two markings alongside the two pieces: a pencil marking to indicate parts which the student is unhappy with and a black biro mark to indicate parts where the student is consciously experimenting in the writing. I'll have all these instructions run off on a sheet, because the students will get to this stage at different times. Many students won't do it because they won't know what it's for — or they won't have thought about experimenting and so on. I'll accept that now, but look for them to do this reflection later in the year.

Then I'll look at the pieces out of lesson and list what I consider to be the most significant strengths of the pieces (what the student can do) and any goals that I might think appropriate. The strengths will be recorded on a semi-official looking form, which has a large box on the left hand side of the page for describing strengths and lines on the right hand side for recording goals. (See examples on pp. 84–85).

Neither my suggested goals nor the students' will be recorded on the form yet. First, I'll talk to the student about the strengths, making reference to any identified by the student and those which I see. Then, we'll talk about any areas marked by the student as difficulties or experiments, and finally about goals raised by the student and me. Out of this, we'll aim to record one goal on the right hand side of the record form and date it. Hopefully, it will be the goal that the student sees as most important.

Name .. Ruth. Year.11.	
Strengths	Goals
4/3 Makes her own decisions about her writing. Is quite happy to reject suggestions for improvement and explain why she rejects them. Likes to tantalise the reader. She wrote: "I want the reader to think about what I have written for a long time before finally understanding my piece of work."	
24/3 Captures spirit of character in monologue from Macbeth.	24/3 Elaborate with more detailed reference to the evidence from the text.
12/4 Strong, punchy conclusion to monologue on "My Brother Jack". "My life was my hard labour job and my writing the time of enjoyment."	12/4 This goal still needs working on.
	21/4 Much more textual evidence in "Realising too late" on "the Doll". Goal successfully worked on. 21/4 To revise first draft, trying out a more formal style and a discussion of a text, not another monologue.
9/5 Strong dramatic title. Edited her work to make parts clearer and her language more formal. Experimented with imagery and was also prepared to cut unsuccessful attempts from final product. A perceptive conclusion very boldly stated which involved reflecting on the clay and drawing a more general point about relationships and change. Also a clear connection between introduction and conclusion.	9/5 Goal successfully worked on. Rephrased obscure bits and wrote contractions out in full. 9/5 Working on hand-out on reading faster, at home.

Name Greg. Year 11	
Strengths.	Goals.
10/3 Dramatic style. Catchy title "I created the thought." Use of metaphor: "Lady Macbeth was midwife to the embryo. Macbeth's wish to grab the crown." Explored in his writing. Perceptive.	
	14/3 Redraft of Macbeth essay.
	16/3 Done, but left out the best parts! To have next essay in on time.
	23/3. Achieved
12/4 More formal style than previously in first two paragraphs. Paragraphed appropriately. Identified padding in his work.	
21/4 Strong clear conclusion. Formal style is being attempted in parts.	
	5/5 Will hand an essay up bit by bit, so that he can be helped to write a longer, more consistently formal piece.
11/5 Use of side-stepping / boxing metaphors in 'My Brother Jack' essay.	11/5 Introduction submitted and discussed briefly.

My message to the student will be 'I'll be giving particular attention to this aspect in your next piece of writing and I want you to do so as well. Be ready to tell me what you have done, concerning this aspect of your writing'. It might be having experimented, having checked drafts to monitor this aspect or having asked another student (who may have this aspect recorded as a strength) for a response or help. I may also undertake to teach about the aspect identified, if that is practical.

Now, all this will be quite time-consuming. In the past it has taken me ten to fifteen minutes' preparation time and five to ten minutes in class, for each student. The saving grace is that I will only do this intensive assessment once a year. (It would be better to do it more often, but where do we find the time?) Time will be saved later because discussions of subsequent pieces and written comments will concentrate on the identified goal. Of course, further strengths may be noted and these can be added to the form, but this will not happen every time. The main feature of the system is that I virtually guarantee that, in reading the next piece, I will give attention to the aspect of writing identified as the goal or learning point.

So, after the first thorough assessment, the titles of pieces submitted will be recorded, along with the date and a reference to performance in relation to the goal. When the goal has been worked on successfully, the students will see it recorded as a strength and later, a new goal will be recorded.

I hope that doing this will show them that I see importance in what they write and that I care about them, not the caring that is expressed through wishy-washy positive comments (which often transmit to students that one has low expectations of them), but through responding articulately, challengingly and, in the final analysis helpfully to their work.

These were high hopes! How did it work in practice?

The first step, having the students describe what they were able to do using the list of criteria in Table 1, did not work well. For many it was as if it was written in a foreign language, and in a sense it was.

Each question in Table 1 asks the students to read their own work critically, with an ear to a particular aspect of what they are reading. Because these students were so unused to doing that, they should have been introduced to the questions one at a time, and given practice at reading in these particular ways. Here were sixteen demanding questions, and the students had no experience of how their answers to them were to be used. So only three of the fifty-two described what they could do in writing, using these questions. Similarly, only six marked on their work parts they were unhappy with and parts where they were experimenting (although those who did got much more specific help when we talked about their writing).

This meant that the initial conversation in which we were to recognize strengths and set goals took longer than I had expected. Ten to fifteen minutes was common and this slowed down our progress through other parts of the course considerably.

Nevertheless, it certainly seemed worthwhile to be spending the time this way, and the examples on pp. 84–85 indicate how the cards were used up to the end of Term 1.

When, a week or so after the first talk, we asked the students what their strengths and goals were, they could remember them and they also referred to them if we asked them to describe their writing. The

Table 1

A. (Overall structuring of information)
1. Have I made the main idea of the piece clear and strong? Will the reader understand the main idea the way I do? Will it be remembered tomorrow?
2. Have I made it clear why what I've written is important? Is the reader likely to see the importance of it?
3. Do some parts need to be explained more? Is the reader left with doubts, confusions or unanswered questions?
4. Are there parts that are unnecessary or hard to see why they are there?

B. (Structuring within the piece)
5. Does the beginnning attract and hold attention, as well as adequately introduce the piece?
6. Does the end seem fitting
7. Are the paragraphs coherent?
8. Do the paragraphs flow from one to the next?

C. (Control of style to keep the reader interested)
9. Is there enough detail for the reader to see or believe in what is presented?
10. Are the words that have been chosen appropriate, strong, precise or is there repetition, clichés, vagueness or silly jargon?
11. Is sentence form and length appropriately varied?
12. Is the title suitable?

D. (Care in presentation)
13. Is the grammar appropriate? (subject–verb agreement, noun–pronoun agreement, it is clear who pronouns refer to?)
14. Is the punctuation appropriate?
15. Is the spelling correct?
16. Is it neat enought to be read fluently?

following comments indicate the range of opinions expressed by the students when they evaluated the strengths and goals approach:

It gives you something to go for in your writing. When you get an essay back you find out something you've done. You feel as if you've achieved something, which is better than being put down all the time.

They're good. You can always check on your goals and what you're good at.

I don't know. I don't think it helps me much. I suppose it makes you think about it. I can't spell. It's not helping me to spell.

It's all right to have a goal but sometimes it's hard to know how to set out to achieve the goal. You need to have that clarified first. The goal I'm trying for now is 'to be succinct' and I'm not sure how to go about it.

Overall, the system seemed to be worthwhile, but as my visits to the school became less frequent, I wondered how it would continue. It had been hard work with two teachers. How could one keep it going? As we had been setting it up, I had recorded how I was feeling about it and this selection from my notes suggests both the promises and the demands of this approach.

- I'm feeling very positive about this. I can think of ten who have done a goal and initiated new goals themselves. And it's near the end of the hard work of getting the procedure going. I feel I am contributing to their writing. The kids do feel accountable. Each kid I've talked to has adopted a goal. I think they all have a sense of direction and I have too.

- Sometimes the process is fairly directive. Otherwise it would take too long. I think they're quite comforted to be given the direction. I think many kids will learn to do it themselves by, at first, simply getting used to the idea of having a goal.

- We've had some success stories in the last few days. For example, Sue had said she couldn't think of a goal and I said 'Well, let's not rush it. We can leave it for a while.' A few days later she said her goal was to make her conclusion strong and punchy. Later she told me she couldn't do it, but when she handed her work up the conclusion was fantastic.

- I notice I go through far more detail, when I talk to them, than I need to. I could just concentrate on the goal.

- If I were taking these classes on my own I think I'd get to talk to between five and ten kids a week, which would mean some kids would be seen only once a month! Maybe that's enough for it to be worthwhile, especially if I refer to their goals in written comments four or five times a term.

- When we talk about their goals it's going well. Without exception they remember them. I'm now working on teaming them up more, so that their goal is often a contract to get specific help from a particular student or to give it.

- The belief that they *can* learn, puts a terrific strain on the teacher. You think 'If only I could get to them more. Offer them the right experiences'. And then you've got them there for a few minutes and you think 'God, where do I start?' No wonder so many teachers decide its's mainly ability: 'those who aren't writing essays couldn't do it anyway'. It would ease your conscience.

- I've just read sixteen kids' work and looked at how they've gone on their goals in an hour, which isn't too bad really. Certainly having the goals there makes it so much easier to read their work.

- I'm noticing that it's important not to focus too much on errors. I think the best goals are often bigger things than focussing on a problem directly. For example, with Gerald we've got a goal which relates to how he'll read and think about the text: just to say to him that he should write less superficially is no good. It's how he's reading that's important.

Here are Sr. Margaret's comments on the system (addressed to me): first, a comment made early in the second term and then a comment near the end of that term.

As a class teacher, I've got quite a tension in relation to this system. It could be the crucial thing whereby a teacher with authority passes over to the student their responsibility for their own learning. They have a goal, they know what they intend to do, they give work to the teacher who informs them of her reaction to what they've written. That to me is a marvellous passing over to the proper person, the authority for her own development.

Also when I had to write the reports, for the first time in my life in English teaching, I felt real about what I was writing, because it actually came out of the goals and strengths. I could dispense with subjective impressions of how they seemed to be in class and concentrate on what they are now attempting to do to develop themselves as writers. That was most satisfying.

On the other hand, as a class teacher I see that I must do bread and butter things. No classroom can have writing done in it until it's an environment in which writing can happen. And so there is this tension between attending to the individual and her motivation and purpose for writing and the big task of ensuring that the whole group is proceeding in some kind of learning.

This week, that tension was deep within me and I simply skimmed over the goals and strengths in favour of maintaining a classroom in which reading and writing could take place.

So I want to retain both those things and quite candidly, I don't know how to do it, when I'm the teacher on my own. But I believe the individual thing is quite crucial.

And nearer the end of term...

> I'm going under with all the end of term pressure. The whole thing about students reflecting on their strengths andgoals is just not happening at the moment, but I still feel quite profoundly that it's right.
>
> When I was working with you I had that support and I chose to do it. I'd been puddling around in a great sea of unknown in three years of English teaching, but this year for the first time I felt I was an English teacher.
>
> Now I'm choosing just to survive and get in what's to be got in. I really regret it.
>
> What that means is that these students are leaving the responsibility for what they learn to other people. How do they know what they should be learning if they're not reflecting on the direction they are going to take? Instead of being self-critical, they're performing for other people and in that they'll always be at sea. They won't advance in self-knowledge which surely is one of the aims of English and writing.
>
> It seems to me that how we set up students' evaluating is half the task of English.

Was what we were trying impractical? Sr. Margaret and I were both new to teaching year 11 English and we were both new to that school. There was a lot we had to get familiar with. My spasmodic attendance at the school did not help either, especially as this system was specifically designed to build a sense of continuity between reflecting and future writing! This system has been used more successfully by Michael Moore at Cleve Area School.

Michael Moore was well established in a smaller, country school and was a very experienced English teacher. He too found that the scheme took a lot of time to get going, but he was using it in all his classes. In the year levels up to year 10 this system completely replaced grading.

On the next two pages are examples of how he used the system. The student record form was stapled to the studen's writing folder.

These records demonstrate the work of a very conscientious teacher: and one who is on top of things. Most, if not all, teachers will sometimes find themselves in a situation where they cannot do such a thorough job. For them a system based on negotiated goals might be too difficult to organize: or it may just have to progress more slowly. One approach would be to begin using Janet Rowe's system for assembling teacher comments and then gradually move to more negotiated goals. Michael referred to 'goals set for her' in one of his reports which suggests that he allowed himself to direct the students to goals at times.

Another possibility is provided by Marion Burn of Plympton High School, who adapted this approach to a student-centred programme, where goal-setting was the students' responsibility.

STUDENT RECORD FORM

NAME: _Cathy_ _Year 9_

Term _III_ Pge 1.

Strengths	Goal and Date
① Imaginative - original ideas	15/9/82 — _'oneness'_ _'individuality'_
② Direct speech.	① Try to be original both description.
③ Appropriate language for given situations.	20/9/82 ② Incorporate concept of 'theme' in writing
④ Strong, effective characterization	12/10/82
⑤ Sentence / Paragraph structure	③ Expand sentences and paragraphs.
⑥ Punctuation.	16/10/82 ④ Experiment with colon and semi-colon.

Writing completed after initial assessment.

Title	Date	Comment
Private Detective	20/9	- Good language control - Interesting variation. - Description ✓✓
Kylie's Heart	30/9	- Soppy - Message about drugs ✓ - theme (simplistic)
Guardian Angel	4/10	- Theme v/strong ✓✓ - Careful with paragraphs - introduction unwieldy
Sounder (Novel response)	12/10.	- Overused short sentence - experimenting. - Conveyed understanding of novel.
Untitled (adoption)	16/10	- touching (not soppy) - short sentences used appropriately
Book Review "Time Tangle"	19/10	- Totally involved with main character - Commented on theme / imagery. - Used semi-colon successfully.

STUDENT RECORD FORM

NAME: _Gavin_   Year 12

Term III   Pge 1.

Strengths	Goal and Date
① Understanding of literature.	24/9
② Logical argument - with examples.	① Express personal response
③ Very wide reading.	28/9
④ Confident ideas & approach.	② Control time spent on essay
⑤ Planning and structure.	1/10 Apostrophe.
	③ Write time over 50 mins at end of essay.
	7/10
	④ Double check for possible opposite interpretations

Writing completed after initial assessment.

Title	Date	Comment
Extension (Shakespeare)	24/9	- Strange interpretation in - Macbeth (discussed) - Hamlet - Totally impersonal.
Judith Wright (Shadow of Death)	28/9	Class essay incomplete. - finished with extra 15 minutes.
My Bro. Jack (Davy's life moulded by his childhood)	28/9	- Well argued - good examples.
Hopkins (Impact of his themes)	1/10	- Apostrophe aggice ^sp. - well over time / length. 65 min
Crucible (Abigail evil?)	1/10	- Apostrophe again - Time improving 55min - Suggest re-write.
Peking	7/10	- Only viewed answer from one side.

STUDENTS SET THEIR OWN WRITING GOALS

At the end of first term, Marion collected the English books from her year 9 class, read through them and, for each student, recorded the strengths she observed in their writing on a 'Writing Achievement Record'. She also noted goals which she thought would be appropriate for each of them. She recorded these in her own work book, but not on the Achievement Record at this stage. This took her about four hours for the class of twenty-four students.

Marion commented on how valuable it was for her to look for strengths in all the student's work:

> I became aware of strengths in some kids' writing, where normally I just hadn't appreciated their style. Also with kids who didn't complete their work or were disruptive, I saw more strengths in their writing than I expected.
>
> One kid was an atrocious speller. It's what you noticed most about his work, but in fact, I saw that he was very articulate and he had a very wide vocabularly. I wrote down some of the words he was using: irate, indiscreet, words like that.

Marion was also led to question her own ability to help some students:

> I'm not very good at working out goals for good writers. I produce fairly trivial ones for them. I'm not really clear at how to extend their writing. And I'm worried about them because I see a lot of students like this at Year 11 who haven't progressed since Year 9.

Early in the second term she handed out the Acievement Records and the students stuck them into their books. Then she got the class into pairs to do three things. Firstly, they were to identify, to their partner, examples from their writing of the strengths Marion had described. The partners were also encouraged to help and Marion circulated, offering her assistance. Marion found that 'Some useful work was done, but many found it too difficult to understand the language used in my comments on their strengths'.

Their second task was 'to work out two goals which you think are important for you to work towards'. Marion referred them to a poster of criteria, very similar to Table 1. The poster had been in the classroom for most of first term and the students had been asked to comment on their own work in relation to those criteria, one at a time, several times during the term. She encouraged them to 'look beyond the mechanics, like spelling and punctuation'.

Their third task was to write these goals in their book on the right hand side of the Writing Achievement Record, and to hand that up for Marion to consider.

Checking on their goals didn't take long: only an hour for the whole class. Most of the kids' goals matched what I had written for them. Some set goals which illuminated for me areas they found difficult — which I hadn't been aware of before. That was very helpful.

With three disruptive students I had been thinking that they might have as a goal simply to complete set work. They set themselves that goal. They took it seriously and they've done it.

In some cases I listed extra goals for them. There were only two kids who'd written goals which I completely disagreed with. These were Ellen and Sonia. Ellen had written only one goal: 'To make my writing neat enough to be read fluently'. I thought it already was. I think she found it very difficult to understand the task, to figure out for herself what she needed to do. I told her I thought her writing was fluent enough to be read clearly and I suggested three things which I thought she could work on: keeping her tenses consistent, correcting her spelling and adding more detail to her work. I asked her to let me know what she thought of these suggestions and she agreed with them.

Sonia had listed two goals (1) 'to use vocabulary better' and (2) 'to think before just writing any old thing'. I didn't reject these ideas but I wasn't too clear about how she intended to achieve them, particularly the second one. I don't think it's necessarily a bad thing to write 'any old thing' in the first place. What I thought she needed was some suggestions about how to revise her work. So I said 'I'm not sure how you're going to achieve (1)' and for (2) I suggested she could reach the goal of writing better by revising her work before writing a final copy and looking for such things as spelling and keeping tenses consistent, and reading it aloud. She agreed to this.'

How are the goals worked on? Marion reminds students to think about their goals, sometimes before they write, and more frequently when they are ready to redraft selected pieces for grading. Many of the goals relate to checking and polishing final copy work.

Some of the goals concern trying different writing tasks to get away from an habitual style and Marion has introduced new tasks for this purpose.

She asks the students to indicate on written work which goals they consider they have achieved, and then she comments on their work specifically in terms of goal achievement.

The main thing about this system is that it gives me criteria to look for that the kids are aware of. We've got a common language. That's superb because so often before comments meant nothing to them.

Each time I look at their books I see if they've achieved any of their goals. I comment specifically on them 'You seem to have made progress on your first goal', and so on. I see progress and it's easy. Everyone has made progress on at least one goal.

The relevance of a few of the goals was diminished when we changed to different writing tasks.

The list of strengths remains useful because I don't lose track of what they can do. And I've been able to use both their strengths and goals when I write reports.

When I talked to the students, most praised the system. They could remember only one or two of their recorded strengths. When we looked them up they could give examples of about half those listed.

However almost all the students could remember their goals, which had been stressed more in the teaching, and could report how they worked on those that concerned reworking and polishing.

Tracey provided an example:

One of my goals was to read my work through and make sure of the endings on words. Here's a piece where I found I'd left the endings off quite a few. I wrote it out again and pasted it over the top of the other.

I asked the students who had proof reading goals, like these, how they came to choose them. They usually referred to Marion or their parents having pointed out that they needed to attend to those aspects.

The students rarely set themselves larger goals concerned with production rather than polishing. When they did, they often chose things they were already doing, for eample, 'to write humorous stories'. It can be useful for the student to have as a goal to refine and gain further confidence in a strength but I felt that the success of the system was limited because the students were not practised at reading to find strengths and goals of a larger kind. Nevertheless, the advantage of it was that the students took responsibility to check apects of their work which had been called to their attention.

Steve Dowdy's approach, which generates writing goals from students' reading (Chapter Four) and the approaches to reading one's own work (Chapter Five) are ways of strengthening students' ability to set themselves goals which go beyond proof reading. When those approaches are used, teachers can be confident that students will develop larger goals. the systems presented in this chapter can then be used to focus the teacher's comments on the goals.

Some teachers who particularly value self-assessment ask students to **record** their own assessments of their writing. Of course many teachers would find such a task very difficult and it is near impossible for students who have not been taught to read critically and who have not received articulate feedback from their teachers. In that too common situation, it is probably a waste of time to ask students to record self-assessments.

On the other hand, when students have learnt to read critically and to apply those ways of reading to their own work, the exercise can help them affirm and celebrate their achievements in writing, as is shown in the next chapter.

7 Helping Students to Assess Their Own Written Products

If it is true that many students are not practised at reading their own work to identify strengths and goals which go beyond the surface features, then this is an area for concern, because these students will remain dependent on others for evaluation of their work.

The previous chapters suggest ways in which students can be taught to read their work for this purpose. The teacher can also monitor the students' ability to read their own work by getting them to write descriptive self-assessments concerning their own writing. Difficulties which often arise with this are well illustrated in the report of Janet Rowe's system on pp. 77–82. The students saw little point in restating her comments in their own words. Either they had understood them, in which case paraphrasing seemed unnecessary, or they had not and needed to ask her what she meant. That there was no external audience for their own versions of the comments made the task of writing them down seem trivial. Whenever the teacher's comments are the main or most authoritative source of evidence about the students' writing, there is the danger that they will think that a self-assessment means simply rehashing the teacher's comments.

Another common way of stimulating students to describe their own writing is to show them the criteria they should address. The questions in Table 1 (p. 87) have been used in that way. However, this can result in an exercise which subjugates their writing to a pre-determined and standardized set of mechanical rules. While the criteria in Table 1 can be useful reference points for reflecting on writing, they are not a solid basis from which a student can write a coherent self-assessment, unless the student has had a lot of experinece of reading for those features. If such a list of criteria has been trotted out especially for the purpose of the self-assessment exercise, the student is being asked to use another's language, as the following examples from year 9 students illustrate:

> The areas which I have to concentrate on are choosing a good title which fit the title perfectly. Also I don't know how to start off a story.
> When I start off with a beginning sentence I write for as long as I want.
> My other parts like Interest and Mechanics are good. In my next piece of writing I must start my work off with the relationship of the title.

> In my opinion, I think that I should concentrate on a proper title for the essay in a manner that I should read the essay and find a proper title that fits the essay.
> I should also concentrate on an opening sentence which should lead on into a paragraph and also a conclusive last paragraph which should sum up the whole essay, which should end up in a statement, fact, or an answer to a question.

These students are focusing primarily on the suggested criteria for writing, whereas their principal focus should be on their **reading** of their work.

Despite these problems, the task of students putting together a written assessment of their own writing appeals to teachers who believe that they should encourage students to think consciously of themselves as writers and to be proud of the specifics of their achievements. Further, written self-assessments can consolidate learning, identify challenges and give students practice at presenting themselves. Such a self-assessment is a required part of **English B**, a Victorian year 12 Higher School Certificate course, written by David McRae with his students at Melbourne State College. The course description[1] suggests that 'a good self-assessment does not imply that all qualities of good writing have been achieved. It simply requires honesty and perception about the qualities and nature of one's own work'. Honesty and perception require that the students be using a language which they can control.

In English B, students write self-assessments because they are required to do so to successfully complete the course. No audience is suggested, and although one could imagine parents, the principal, or a moderator being proposed, there is usually no audience for the self-assessments. Yet English B to some extent avoids the problems of students regurgitating the teacher's comments or relying on a set of questions phrased in a 'foreign' language. In English B their self-assessments are grounded in their own experience, and in particular, their experience of reading other authors.

Jo Hall of Greenwood High School prepares her non-academic students for writing self-assessments through two other required aspects of the writing unit in English B, 'writing analysis' and a 'statement about good writing'. The students use what they learn in these two sections of the course when they write their self-assessments. I will describe how Jo handles these two activities and then present an example of the self-assessments that result.

WRITING ANALYSIS

Students are expected to do between ten and fifteen writing analyses during the year and then to sit a test involving two unseen pieces. They take the test when they are ready to. They can use notes as a guide and can express their analysis in writing or orally. Most choose to write it. If they fail the test, they are taught some more and allowed to repeat it. 'This activity is designed to identify some of the elements of craft that writers bring to bear on their work.'[2]

Jo chooses the pieces to be discussed by her class. At first she chooses pieces from magazines like *TV Week* and from students' writing from other classes. Later in the year she concentrates on more difficult, editorial style articles from newspapers like *The Age*. In between, use is made of textbooks, established literature and commercial writing. Students can be involved in selecting passages for analysis, both pieces they think are good and pieces they think are bad.

Jo: The biggest problem early on is that they focus on the writing, a little bit at a time. They don't see the forest for the trees. So we start off in a broad way, discussing type of writing and audience and purpose. That means they don't focus too narrowly and mechanically.

After that an important question is 'How can you tell?' So it's not just, 'What is the audience?' but also 'How do you know?'. That involves focussing in on vocabulary, sentence construction and so on.

So, early in the year, Jo and the class discuss different audiences for writing, and together develop a list of attributes which suggest what the intended audience for a piece of writing is. This leads on to exercises such as the following:

Audience: Examine each of the items listed below, in the library, and suggest for whom the author(s) were writing. Define audience by age, educational level, background, interests, membership of sub-groups, and occupation.
  1. 'Looking at China'
  2. 'The World of Chemistry'
  3. 'Vogue' magazine (April)
  4. 'The Bulletin'
  5. 'Ecos'

6. 'Everywoman'
7. 'Pernod'
8. 'The Work Book'
9. 'Australian Politics'
10. 'The Age' newspaper (any edition)
To determine audience, look at difficulty of language, topic, tone, advertisements, stated aims (if any), pictures, how deeply topics are investigated, format, size of writing, length of articles.

Later on, Jo provides the students with questions to guide their consideration. For example, one class was given five short extracts from newspapers, a magazine and a text-book. They were to answer these questions in small groups:

(1) What is it?
(2) What is the intended audience? How can you tell?
(3) What was the writer's aim (or aims)?
(4) What techniques did the writer use?
(5) How successful is it, in view of your answer to (2) and (3)? Explain your assessment.

As the year goes on the aspects of writing that are considered in class are collated onto a 'Step-by-step guide to successful writing analysis'. This lists aspects of writing that the students have discussed. Here is an extract from the 'Step-by-step guide' produced from one class's discussions.

1. Identify the form used.
2. Description of probable intended audience and comment on this piece of writing's suitability for that audience.
3. Discussion of what the writer was trying to achieve. Some aims might be: to persuade people to his/her point of view; to amuse; to shock; to educate; to share an important experience; to persuade readers to buy something; to provoke a feeling reaction of anger, disgust, passion, sympathy; to let others know how he/she feels and thinks; to create something beautiful; to raise readers' awareness of some issue.
3. (a) Examine the techniques used by the author to achieve his/her aims: Some commonly used techniques are:
   (1) maintain interest, varying sentence structure and type — using direct speech, short and long sentences, exclamations, rhetorical questions.
   (2) using evocative words and phrases, or emotion-laden ones. (Give examples).
   (3) using examples calculated to arouse certain emotions in the reader.

(4) using case histories as illustrations, to lead readers to identify with the characters.

(5) using double meanings of words or phrases to amuse or stimulate the reader.

(6) using powerful, original imagery; including similes and metaphors.

(7) putting things in an amusing way.

The main teaching for 'writing analysis' comes from students combining their comments to form one analysis from a small group.

Jo: Later I get them to do it individually at home, in writing. I might comment on them or get other kids to. They get to know what's expected.

Some catch on to writing analysis very quickly. Others have trouble, but by the end of the year they can all say something relevant that they wouldn't have been able to say at the beginning of the year.

The teacher who takes the Higher School Certificate Group One course, English Literature, has said that kids doing this course seem to be advantaged when they come to literary analysis.

The tests for writing analysis usually involve material that comes from the school context, for example, a notice to parents and a poem in the school magazine.

STATEMENT ABOUT GOOD WRITING

Along with 'writing analysis', the 'statement about good writing' also prepares students to be able to describe their own writing. It is also done because it is a requirement of the course. There is no audience for it other than the class and teacher. The course description suggest that

the purpose of this is to bring to consciousness what is often left to intuition. Although we cannot precisely define for all time what good writing is, we can make a solid effort to bring certain characteristics into focus.

It is the business of the class and the teacher to find suitable terms, that seem for them to be explicit and appropriate. The preparation of this statement is not a matter of seeing how close one can come to whatever statements of received opinion exist concerning good writing. The development of this statement should be a corporate enterprise, entailing discussion.

For the purposes of assessment students should be able to describe their contribution to its preparation.[3]

Early in the year, Jo gets the class to brainstorm qualities of good writing. I saw several records of these sessions. Characteristics listed included:

- Lets you know and feel what the good and bad sides of life really are.

- Informs you about something you want to know.

- Takes a familiar idea and changes it into something interesting.

- It is rounded off with a satisfying and interesting ending.

- Must create a desire to drink milk.

- Good if it shows people escaping danger.

- Goals to strive for — must show people striving for goals and succeeding.

Jo reports:

There are a few disagreements early on. When we come back to it in the second half of the course, they know the statement is basically up to them. I could feed ideas into the discussion, but I don't usually. In their brainstorms they cover as many things as I cover.

Concensus must be acheived on the final statement. They have wanted to have voting to get it over quickly, but I won't accept that.

Near the end of the year I spend a lesson going round getting everyone to give specific examples of how they contributed and they can do that. As with the rest of this course, they have to have been fully involved, to be assessed as having satisfactorily completed the course.

Here is an example of a final statement:

Good writing statement

Good writing mut have a heading which catches the reader's eye. The writing must be relevant to the topic. If facts are used they must be accurate. The topic, language, size of print and length of paragraphs must be suited for its intended audience. Spelling, grammar and punctuation must be correct, except when the conventions are broken for a special effect. All good writing has either a climax or a point. Each sentence must flow and be connected with those before and after it. Sentence structure should be varied. The introduction must encourage the reader to go on. The rest of the piece must keep the reader's interest. The ending must leave the reader feeling stimulated and satisfied.

SELF-ASSESSMENTS

During the year Jo gets the students to practise describing their own writing by completing a cover sheet when they hand up finished work. The cover sheet has headings under which they indicate the audience for the writing, the reason they wrote it, 'What it was like writing it' and an assessment of the piece.

Jo: Early in the year, they were not always very involved in doing these cover sheets, but they are similar to the 'writing analysis' which they're learning how to do. And they see the cover sheets as recording information for the self-assessment statement that is required by the end of the course.

Here is a cover sheet, completed by Silvina, about a poem she wrote.

NAME: Silvina Glattaver
TITLE: Death by human selfishness
AUDIENCE: Anybody interested in poetry from the ages 14 and above
REASONS FOR WRITING IT:
I like conveying thoughts through poetry. War is a subject which interests me.
WHAT IT WAS LIKE WRITING IT:
It didn't take long because the words came easily and the topic is interesting. I liked using single words to convey an image.
MY ASSESSMENT OF THIS PIECE OF WRITING:
This is a good poem because it conveys two aspects of war — on the battlefield and at home. There is a good variation of sentence structure to make the poem more interesting. I think the last stanza is especially good because it is a sum up of the result of war.

Near the end of the year the students apply what they have learnt in 'writing analysis' and the 'statement on good writing' to their own writing.

Jo: When it's time to do the final self-asessment, they've done stacks of writing analysis and they use the guide sheet from that for their self-assessments. I summarize the criteria which have come up in 'writing analysis' on the blackboard in a discussion of what to look for, and we put more stuff in as well (e.g. clichéd theme).

A partner reads all their work, which takes a couple of lessons, and tries to pick up general things. Feedback they get from audiences is also included. Mostly this is from people their own age or younger.

I get them to reread their finished writing and to look at the statement on good writing. It's supposed to be taken into account too.

> They write a first draft of their self-assessment and I expect about
> a page. I look at the draft and I ask for specific examples of what they
> say. For example, if they say 'It could have been more interesting', I
> ask 'How would you make it more interesting?'.

The self-assessments confirm and celebrate the students' learning.
Here is an excerpt from Silvina's seven page self-assessment: this
excerpt refers specifically to a five hundred word piece she wrote, titled
— 'A Ride on the Thunderbolt Roller-Coaster'. It was Silvina's idea to
set her self-assessment out this way.

AUDIENCE: 14–15 years who have ridden on this ride or plan to.
FORM: creative description
STYLE: descriptive, humorous
— The heading of this piece indicates what it is about, therefore
appealing to the reader.
— The rest of the piece is all relevant to the topic.
— The facts are all accurate, as it is my own experience.
— The topic, language, size of print and length of paragraphs are suited
for its intended audience although some of this is complex.
— Spelling, grammar and punctuation are all correct.
— The climax in this piece of writing is the few lines which cover the
acctual ride.
— Good use of imagery—there is a lot all the way through—e.g.
simile—'took off like a rocket on fire', **metaphorical
personification**—'Hiding behind trees it seemed to reach the
heavens. We walked over to this staring monster which seemed to say
…', **metaphor**—'my stomach fell out'.
— Sentence structure is sometimes complex to suit this type of writing
e.g. 'My stomach fell out as we turned upside down and then coming
down full force, we entered the second loop.'
— the introduction encourages the reader to read on because it sets the
scene of where, when and why this event was taking place.
— The rest of the piece keeps the reader's interest because one thing
leads to another and the reader has to keep reading to the end to find
out what happens.

Jo's work provides an example of how a teacher can help students to
write self-assessments based on their reading of their work. I have
quoted typical, rather than model examples. They do not completely
avoid the situation where students are using a language which is not
their own, but they are more grounded in the students' experience than
most self-assessments written in schools.

If students practised these approaches to reading their own and
published work at various levels of their schooling, they would gradually

develop a sense of accomplishment based on their knowledge of what they have achieved in writing, not on their teachers' evaluations of them.

We have seen that helping students reflect on their writing involves focusing on how they read. In the next chapter, we turn to helping students reflect on their reading.

8 Helping Students to Reflect on Their Reading

In Chapter One I argued that students do not learn writing simply through having many experiences of doing it. To learn to control the medium they also must reflect, conceptualize and experiment. A similar situation applies with reading. Bryant Fillion suggests:

> Certainly one characteristic of 'good readers of literature' is their willingness and ability to consider and think about what they have read, and about its effect on them. It is not enough just to have the experience, we must also consider its meaning. It is perhaps through a growth in reflectiveness that learners of literature benefit most.[1]

Students see little point in reflecting on their reading when they think that reading is simply a matter of passively absorbing the correct interpretations: they often think that the teacher or another expert could simply provide them with the right meanings. Reflecting on reading is important precisely because it contradicts that understanding. In reflecting the reader acknowledges that he has some responsibility for and power over the creation of his own litrary experiences. So just as we can help students think about what they are **doing** when they write (Chapter Four), so we can help them think about what they are **doing** when they read.

There is an exciting paradox in what reflection involves in English. While teaching students to reflect on their **writing** involves teaching them to **read** it in the role of the audience, teaching students to reflect powerfully on their **reading** involves teaching them to approach texts in the role of a **writer**, or at least, as someone who can authoritatively produce language about a world which relates to that described in the text.

When students can see similarities between the texts they read and language which they have produced (be they similarities in content or form), they have a reference point from which they can evaluate the texts. Without this reference point, they are hard pressed to reflect on the texts, because the language needed to do so is not grounded in their experience. The best they can do is crib others' opinions.

To take a simple example, if you wanted students to be aware of images of death and despair in some poems, you could begin by asking them for images they associate with these things themselves. After arriving at symbols they might use, they will be in a position to evaluate the poet's choices. They will be much less likely to note down 'x is a symbol of despair', as if this represented an inevitable equivalence that one might find in a dictionary of symbols.

Here is an example of a teacher monitoring students' engagement in a text, which illustrates how powerful their reflection becomes when they can play the role of writer.

Bill Greenwell got a class to make up thirty characters. Through various activities, they developed personalities for their characters, practised presenting them ironically and finally took them on a voyage on which they interacted and told each other stories. All this was preparatory to reading The General Prologue to *The Canterbury Tales*, and when they got to it...

> The barrier of 14th century English was broken. Reading from the original, and without any preparation for the language, the group were in tune with the wry, sprightly irony of the narrator. They laughed at, rocked along with and grasped the mood of the piece without any teacherly prompting. They knew what Chaucer was about, becuase they had been about the same business. Lengthy teacher-exposition disappeared and discussion was stimulating, well-motivated and informed.[2]

This example both impresses and intimidates me. If monitoring students' engagement with a text involves **observing how** they relate their own language to the text, how do English teachers do that? In the rest of this chapter I describe the work of English teachers who do this; who concentrate on monitoring and encouraging students' production of language in response to the text. I discuss how they monitor what the students are **doing** as they express their responses, under the headings used in Chapter Four getting language going, exploring and discovering, choosing and rejecting, experimenting and anticipating readers' needs.

GETTING LANGUAGE GOING

Students respond to texts in many ways: through their senses (for example, when they visualize a scene or character), emotions and intellect; and in action. Some of their most important responses may never be verbalized. English teachers hope that students will deepen their responsiveness to texts at all levles: for example, teachers often show students what excites them in a text, by reading it aloud. When it comes to monitoring the students' exploration and engagement in the text, English teachers usually **concentrate** on how students can use language to express and deepen their responses. So the English teacher monitors the flow of language about the world of the text, in each student. This is not the language of literary criticism, but language of their own which complements that used by the writer. Only with an awareness of a larger world of possible, related uses of language, does a reader gain perspective on what the writer chose to do (whether or not these choices were deliberate). Lola Brown provided a clear example of that when her students devised their 'love map' before reading Donne (Chapter Three, page 24). After making the map, the students were in a position to consider the attitudes of love which Donne expressed, not as an inevitable selection, but as attitudes he **chose** to write about, from a wider set of possibilities.

In Chapter Five I suggested that the flow of a reader's language can be tapped by easing the intellectual demand on the reader, that is, by not asking for a processed comment on the work as a whole, but rather for a sharing of more particular reactions. So the emphasis will often be on monitoring the flow of language during reading, not just at the end.

To get this less processed language flowing, Patricia Murphy, of Manu High School, gets groups of students from years 6 to 11 to translate poems into a dramatic performance. She emphasizes[3] that 'the urgency and pressure of a drama preparation time facilitated contributors. The group knew a product was wanted, soon ...' and that 'the task of dramatization emphasizes the visual aspect of the poems and makes the imagery a concrete phenomenon that the students can see and manipulate'.

Poetry and short stories are often the focus of reflection on reading. Because they are accessible as whole pieces they lead quickly to discussion of the particular, which can include organisational aspects of the text. The technique of 'showing how you read' (Chapter Five) can be applied to short literary pieces. The instructions which I used required students to identify 'overload' and 'underload', and they are important when reading texts: skilled readers reflect on the demands the writing is making of them and adjust their reading rate accordingly, whereas less skilled readers read at a uniform ate, with little monitoring of their own level of comprehension.

With longer texts, Jim Dellitt of Parafield Gardens High School gets students to keep a reading diary, an approach which he suggests 'allows students space to "pluck out the heart of the mystery"'. Jim read *Hamlet* with a year 11 class ....

A diary was kept by each student and by me. The entries were alternately personal reactions to parts of the play and Hamlet – imagined comments; both were written in the first person. The student-as-Hamlet entries could be in modern language, though bits of the play could be incorporated if the student was comfortable with them .... I believe the student must have space to develop a personal response and the teacher needs to be aware of this response before it is focussed or rerouted by his teaching.[4]

Jim commented on the language of the students' journal entries:

What became interesting was that the imagery and language of the play emerged in their writing, for example ...
'Ah! finally rid of that old fool Polonius. But is death the only way to rid yourself of a nuisance? ... yet it appalls me so to see one make such a fool of oneself.' (Shane).

Heather Carey of Salisbury East High School used Jim's idea, again with students reading *Hamlet*. They kept a journal as if they were Hamlet, and Heather noticed that

in the formal essays which followed journal writing, the students were able to interweave the language of the play with their own thoughts. Their use of quotations improved considerably in both relevance and sentence construction and I feel that this was a direct result of the fact they were using their inside knowledge, rather than working from a detached, uninvolved position.[5]

Heather saw many students developing their control over language which had been stimulated by the text. For example, one student wrote in her *Hamlet* journal,

I have a reluctance, which I myself can acknowledge, to take positive action ... Oh the time is out of joint — Oh cursed spite that ever I was born to set it right. Why should all this incest, corruption and murder come to this land at this time? How will I ever be able to deal with it?

David Harris of The Heights School allows his students to choose the texts they will write about. So his approach has to be much more individualized. At all year levels he gets the students to write down 'ten things you are thinking in relation to the text' — rather like a brainstorm.

At first, in the junior secondary years, these points tend to be merely a record of what occurred in the text. David then talks to the students about their lists, reinforcing what they have done and suggesting that they also consider other aspects of the text (for example, setting, characters' motivations or the writer's purpose). Fay read *Lord of the Flies* and her list was simply a summary of events:

(1) Crashed on an uninhabited island.
(2) Built a fire to get rescued and attract ships. Called assemblies with a conch.
(3) Little boy was burned in bush fire.
(4) Built huts and shelters to sleep in....

                                                                    and so on.

When David talked to her he emphasized considering **why** the events happened. In her subsequent essay, Fay made a concerted attempt to explore that question, finishing with

> In some parts of the story, I felt like jumping into the book and sorting out Jack once and for all. I felt angry.

By year 12, this list 'of ten things' are a mixture of highly selected, critical events, interpretations of theme and connections with other works. For example, Alison read *The Mayor of Casterbridge* and *Tess of the D'Urbevilles* and wrote these twenty points:

Hardy — 20 major points

1. Moral values.
2. Women less significant than men.
3. People and society, social status.
4. Religion.
5. Coincidence.
6. Sex outside of marriage — bastards looked down on.
7. Effect of industrial revolution. Women, cheap labour.
8. Wessex, confined to one area.
9. Importance of handshake as a deal.
10. Social outcasts.
11. Symbolism.
12. Withold of secrets and how the person was destroyed by them.
13. Superstition.
14. Build up and breakdown of characters.
15. Marrying into money.
16. Evils of drink — Marion, Tess's father and Henchard.
17. Widespread poverty.
18. Hardy writes from a woman's point, Bronte's from a male.
19. Henchard tragic like Macbeth.
20. Attitudes to sex — prudish.

After talking over this list with David, she wrote a thousand word essay on the status of women in Hardy's novels.

The teaching approaches referred to in this section (word trees, translating a text into a group drama presentation, 'showing how you read', a reading diary, diary from a character's point of view and the 'lists of what you are thinking') are powerful ways of stimulating students to reflect on their reading. They can be used before, during and after the reading of a text.

EXPLORING AND DISCOVERING

After considering the students' initial reflections, the teacher can then challenge them to explore and discover more about the issues they raised. Here are three ways teachers do this.

When David Harris's students have made their lists he talks to them individually.

> A big part of what I do while I'm talking with them, is to wait, to hold off, till something clicks — till I've got an intuitive sense that they've found an idea which gives them excitement and discovery. I can see in their face when we've got there.
>
> But, sometimes I jump in and give them a topic. It's all very intuitive. Whatever rule I tell you, I actually break. I hear Jane talking about a problem with her boyfriend and it comes! I've got a topic that relates to what she's been reading and I set it. There's no great danger because if it's not right for her she won't do it anyway.
>
> Sometimes I get insane games going to provoke them to manipulate the text. Eve-Marie in year 10, has read *Jane Eyre* and *Travels with my Aunt*. As a challenge, and entirely spontaneously, I told her to incorporate a country dunny into her writing about each of them: and it must be a rational, unobtrusive part of the essay. If I notice it, she fails, If I don't she gets an A: She's done it quite well with *Jane Eyre*: 'The fog was thick, and the carriage stopped, not, as you would expect, in front of the house, but …'. That was just a private game we played that day. No rational, serious, defensible motive. It just happened and we enjoyed the fun.
>
> Sometimes I'm autocratic. If they choose texts which I think are weak I'm more likely to set the question. Chris in year 9 read six Mills and Boon romance stories. So I set her questions that push her to consider that world. 'Compare this story with what you see happening around you', 'Talk about the kinds of loving there are, and which are in this book', and 'Will you have a happy ending in the love stories of your life?'.

The topic decided upon during this talking must be one which David sees value in, and it just not be similar to another student's topic in that class. Later, they will broaden their knowledge of texts by reading each other's writing. The talking takes between ten and twenty minutes for each student. David's commitment to the student's personal choice is so great that he gives this time instead of teaching the whole class at once.

As well he accepts that a lot of the time some students do not appear to be doing much in class time. His back-up is that while there are only minimal rules about behaviour in class, he makes demanding requirements on them in terms of the amount of work to be done. These requirements are clearly set out at the beginning of the year and the students are frequently reminded that it is their responsibility to meet them.

> They have to read a set number of books by the end of the year — or else they fail. And they have to write long essays. In Year 10, anything less than four hundred words is unacceptable: in Year 12, a thousand words is the minimum. I keep my marks book open in the class, for them to look at. They can see what they have to do. And they do it. I'm happy with the work they do, and that's the important thing.

The real point is that I too am exploring and discovering my reactions to the book. Nothing remains absolute for long. In this shared exploration of literature, I am continually finding things that are new to me. Basically, it all depends on those pleasant, exciting conversations with students.

Jim Dellitt also takes time to monitor students' initial responses to texts, before he suggests how they might be explored further. He often gets his students to complete sentence starters like these ...

If I were Douglas ...
When I read the bit ...
One part I liked ...
I found it difficult ...
If my mum or dad read this ...

He explained to me how he follows up their responses:

I usually have about ten of these sentence starters. I look over them for something that I think can be developed and refined. Here are two examples from what two year 9 students wrote about *The October Child* by Eleanor Spence.

Alan: If *Carl was my brother* I wouldn't be able to stand him for very long and would eventually leave home.
Douglas was too helpful when it came to helping his mum and dad and often suffered because of it.

Jane: If *Carl was my brother* I would have to be a strong person because I think I would crack.
Douglas was a very strong person, I mean having to cope with a brother like Carl and having all his things broken and chucked around ...

These two responses illustrate interesting reflections by the students. Both Alan and Jane have made tentative analyses of Carl's and Douglas's character and have supported their comments with vague reference to events and relationships. They have also related the novel to themselves and their experience, predicting how they would respond in the situations the novel describes.

I then set individual questions for each student based on their initial responses. As my evaluation of what they've written, I write something like 'I was interested to read that you found Douglas a strong person. Can you define a strong person and relate that definition to Douglas, Carl, the family and yourself?' Often they don't understand. That's all right. They come and ask: that's good.

I might ask Alan to predict if Douglas will leave home and whether that will be a solution to the problems emerging in the novel. I do all this during the reading, not at the end.

Students can also explore and discover by expressing their questions, confusions and doubts about the text. Sr. Margaret Cain and I referred to these as 'puzzlements' in class work and they are down-to-earth versions of the academics' 'problem of ambition in *Macbeth*'.

However it is a dangerous business showing others your questions, for you might be showing them where you are silly or ignorant. If we are to educate we must create a classroom environment where even apparently silly questions are seen as valuable ways of getting discussion and learning going. Otherwise students often mimic the teacher's questions — or copy them from notes of other students — in an attempt to ask the right question.

Explorations can involve taking on the role of a character or the author, either dramatically or in writing. For example, Karen had as her 'puzzlement',

> How could Lady Macbeth sacrifice her femininity and good natured soul to influence the murder of Duncan?

As Lady Macbeth she answered ...

> I want the spirits to take away my womanliness so I will not be soft-hearted. No part of me is to prevent me from committing the murder. I hope the night is so dark that the beautiful heavens will not remind me of God and my conscience. I feel I still have goodness in me so I am calling on evil to repress my goodness. I clearly wish my husband to wear the crown but he will need my influence as he is too kind hearted. I feel I am a tower of strength. With my persuasion, I know Macbeth will see the prophecies through.

In explorations like this students can consolidate deeper understandings of a text than they are likely to develop while in the role of students trying to match teachers' expectations of essay structure and style. As Peter Adams, of Meningie Area School argues; 'We **all** know more than we can tell, and teachers need to provide their students with ways in which they can reveal the kinds of understandings of literature which do not lend themselves to being stated discursively or analytically.'[6]

The teacher's role is to monitor and deepen students' exploration: this can involve observing which aspects of the text the student considers (events, plot, characters, relationships, setting, atmosphere, images, themes or language), and which types of response are expressed (factual, interpretative , personal associations or evaluations).[7] The teacher can then intervene to prompt the student to relate more aspects of the text to an exploration which began with a specific question or issue.

CHOOSING AND REJECTING

A writer develops a sense of the value of a piece by focusing on what seems to work ('This is my main point') and rejecting parts that seem ineffective ('It's better without that part'). The reflective reader does this as well. In the lessons which followed the making of the 'love map' (Chapter Three, p. 24) and reading of Donne's poetry, Lola Brown gave this as the stimulus for the first writing task:

> Of all the poems I've read so far ...... has made the strongest impression on me.

A typical response from a student who did not see herself as good at English, included this paragraph:

> There is another poem which I liked as much as *The Anniversarie* and that is *Song: Goe and catche a falling stare*'. Most of all this poem humoured me, but it also struck me as being quite practical advice for our day. That is what Donne is saying can be placed right in our day, for today it is really hard to find someone who is sincere and who can be trusted with love. Maybe it was the same in Donne's time, but I know from bitter experience that it is really hard to find someone who is really sincere and who can make a relationship last. Even though Donne is exaggerating in his poem, I can place a lot of other people in the place of the 'woman' in the poem. I must also mention that a 'man' can be placed in the place of the 'woman' described. This poem is funny, and exaggerated but it also has a lot of truth in it.

Similarly, a second writing task required the students to **choose** particular lines and images. The stimulus was:

> I remember these lines because ......

> I remember this image because ......

EXPERIMENTING

In a series of articles,[8] Peter Adams of Meningie Area School describes tasks in which students experiment within the framework provided by a specific literary text. This can involve the student extending the imaginative world of the work (for example, in a sequel), rewriting the end of a work or imitating aspects of the original.

These are very demanding tasks. Yet Peter reports that in them, students 'tend to write at greater length' than usual and to 'be more adventurous, more imaginatively daring, as if relieved of a burden that oppressed their creative spirits. In addition, such students are demonstrably learning the "tricks of the trade" from inside — by doing, rather than analysing how someone else did it'.

I suggest in later chapters that the 'burden that oppresses their creative spirits' is the lack of a clear model of what it is they are being asked to do. When students write an imitation or improvisation within a provided structure, it is a demanding task, but the demands are spelt out, and the students can concentrate on meeting them. They are not confused or anxious about what is expected and consequently often write very powerfully. Peter Adams presents many examples. Here is one by James Farmer,[9] a boy in one of Peter's year 9 classes. Peter had asked them to write an epilogue to *Lord of the Flies*, to show how Jack and Ralph and the other boys reacted to being returned to their normal lives in England, after their experiences on the island.

> Jack strolled across the lane, kicking pebbles into the grassy ditch where water gurgled. Rain drizzled, the stone wall draped with moss dripped, and further on, a frog croaked. He stopped to listen to the frog again, and became Jack the hunter. The air was quiet, apart from water trickling and the sound of the road a few blocks away. The frog croaked again, and Jack swept forward, his satchel swaying under his arm. The thought of catching his bus to school did not cross his mind. He was hunting again, and that was all that mattered to him. All his senses were sharp, his eyes missed nothing under the grass where his prey might sit. The hunter's hand skilfully delved beneath the mossy bank of the ditch and he grinned at what lay underneath. A pair of moist, beady eyes peered up from a fat, little body, its fat stomach heaved up and down as it puffed air in and out of its mouth. Jack frowned and grabbed at the ball of fat. The frog hopped into the stream and kicked away. Jack watched it come to rest on a stone. The feeling of being bettered by such a small animal angered him. He breathed in and leapt after the frog. Water splashed his trousers and soaked his shoes. He stumbled on, bending and grabbing at the hopping figure ahead of him. At last he knelt in wet moss, grasping the billowing frog in his fist. None of his anger had subsided, he had power over the fat little frog. Jack rose slowly, his front dripping with water, his breathing heavy. All the frustrations of the past few days at school, in strict civilized society, were let out at once as he hurled the frog at the stone wall. Its body splattered half-way up the wall; its head opened and blood oozed out. 'I meant that', uttered Jack.
>
> James Farmer

Students can also be involved in experimenting by getting them to apply their language directly to a text. David Mallick provides an example where he deletes words and short lines from poems, both published and student work. The students' attempts to replace the missing words 'stimulate vigorous discussion on appropriateness, accuracy, power of words and images, and success of rhythm'.[10] After undertaking these experiments, the students refer back to the original text, not to find the right answer, but to see how their choices compare with the writer's.

ANTICIPATING READERS' NEEDS

Writing about a text to a teacher who is a relative expert on it is often an academic exercise. Rarely is the teacher wanting to learn about the text.

Rather she is usually checking to see if the student can refer to the specifics of the text and at the same time build an argument at a high level of abstraction! It is more a matter of learning a particular style of thinking than anticipating readers' needs.

But the readers' needs can be a focus for deepening reflection on the text. Lola Brown highlighted the sense of writing to an audience when her students wrote their final piece on Donne. The instructions were: 'Use five quotations to give someone who doesn't know Donne's poetry an idea of its unique flavour.' Here is an extract from a three page piece written by the student quoted earlier:

> These two preoccupations bring out also the point that Donne bases his poems on himself, he centres himself as the prominent subject in a lot of the love and religious verses.
>
> In the religious verse he places himself at the centre of attention. His sins are greater than anyone else and he needs to be forgiven more than anyone else — e.g. Holy Sonnet, VII.
>
> 'For, if above all these, my sinnes abound
> 'Tis late to aske abundance of thy grace, …
> Teach mee how to repent';
> In the love poetry the only important people are himself and his lover — they are the centre of their own little world, e.g. 'The Sunne Rising'.
> 'Thou sunne art halfe as happy as wee,
> In that the world's contracted thus,
> …and thou art every where,
> This bed thy centre is, these walls thy sphere.'

Lola commented on this piece:

> Given the context of impending exams, these students recognized this task for what it fundamentally was — an examination type essay on 'characteristics'. The style of writing represented by this piece — where the student's personal voice, obvious in the previous quotation, is missing — was the same, give or take a few degrees of competency, in all the answers. The one new element, by comparison with previous years, was the variety in their choice of quotations and points of reference. That revealed to me a more confident command of the poetry than I had seen before.

David Harris sees his most important role to be as an audience to students **talking** about the text. Often he has not read the book the student has chosen or he cannot remember it clearly. This is particularly common in the junior secondary years.

> I have to show them I'm learning from them: that they're the experts. They are all bright — each one of them. Their illuminations are the cause for much joy.

Once the student has fixed on something to write about,

> I can muck around a bit. I expect the students to admit their prejudices
> and I will too. I'm talking to Debbie about *Jane Eyre*: I say 'I get half way
> through and I think Jane cops out. She's a pain — too proper — irritating
> beyond measure. All that earlier, vigorous independence dissipates. I
> could never finish the book.' But Debbie tells me firmly, 'Jane is getting
> stronger. She has a gentle passion which you mistake' and she goes on to
> prove her point.

What these two teachers are trying to do is deepen the students'
reflections on texts by working to provide them with a real audience —
an audience that wants to know the students' own responses, and which
does not have an expert, model answer in mind. Jim Dellitt operates
similarly when he sets his individualised questions based on the
students' initial responses.

In contrast, when teachers set closed questions which identify what
issues the students must consider, they reinforce in many students the
idea that they must try and match a model answer. For those students,
thinking about the text is more like role-playing the teacher than
consciously making their own discoveries in the world of the text.

Many teachers complain that examinations often focus on narrow
questions. Does that mean that students must be given continual
practice at closed questions? I suspect not. The three teachers just
discussed give students little or no practice at them and each has an
outstanding record of success in terms of their students' results in
traditional, state-wide examinations.

David Harris believes that if students spend a relatively long time
developing one, strong, well thought out and often idiosyncratic
perspective on a text, then they can usually use that as a strong basis
from which to consider other specific issues in the text. His experience
is that this is a more successful strategy than trying to cover a number of
issues which the examiners might choose to focus on.

The approaches described in this chapter can be used across the
range of year levels and texts. Some of the examples here concerned
'high' literature: Shakespeare, Donne, Jane Austen. When they actively
explore connections between the language of their world and the
language of the text, students can be helped to approach a whole range
of writers, including those from previous centuries. Teachers can help
them appreciate what they have in common with established writers,
both in their concerns and their creativity.

9 Helping Students Reflect on Their Oral Language

English classes which I have worked with have had too little time and too many students to be suitable settings for a concentrated, consistent focus on oral language. Reading and writing have been demanding enough — and of course teaching reading and writing involves a lot of listening and speaking.

In Chapter Two I argued against informal and continuous assessment of students' oral language, because students should know what is going to be assessed and be able to prepare for the judgement situation. Nor should we grade or write descriptive reports of students' oral language when there has only been time for one presentation from each student. Students' oral language should not be judged unless we have been helping them to learn the criteria they are likely to be judged on, to monitor their own development, and to prepare a polished presentation for judging.

SHOWING HOW YOU RESPOND

When teachers find themselves able to work seriously on oral language, they can use approaches similar to those discussed in Chapter Five.

Most speaking is intended to have certain effects on the listeners. Teachers can help students understand how they affect their listeners and how they can take listeners' needs into account, by having students and other audiences listen to their talking and respond to it.

Students can show how they respond, as listeners, in **detailed** ways, following instructions like those for 'showing how you read':

- identifying things the speaker said which were strong and made an impact;

- identifying things which were confusing or which they disagreed with;

- identifying when they were overloaded by more information than they knew what to do with;

- identifying when there was too little new information;

and if the material is recorded, the tape can be stopped mid-way and the listeners asked to predict what is to follow.

It is best to start with the open-ended task of students 'showing how they respond', using these guidelines, because then the student listeners are not intimidated by the thought that they have to get **the** correct answer. This means that the speakers get the most natural, and usually the most important, feedback available, that is the range of responses others have when they are simply listening, not playing the role of encourager, instructor or critic.

As 'showing how you respond' is practised in class, students become more conscious of their own listening and, as speakers, more aware of how specific aspects of their talking come across to others. They can also do the activity as listeners to recordings of their own speech.

Through 'showing how you respond', students can give feedback to each other on anything from a formal presentation to the class, to participation in group work, telling a joke or role-playing paticular social situations.

After this very simple approach to listening has been practised, emphasis can be given to helping students respond to a piece of oral language, **as a whole**, following similar guidelines to those presented in the final sections of Chapter Five. The students can express what they find to be:

- the main idea or 'centre' of a piece of language;

- the main elements of the piece;

- the relationships between the main elements;

and also, whether they felt they were **led** to understand the significance of the presentation, perhaps with special focus on how it was introduced.

Then when these ways of responding as listeners have been solidly established, the teacher can introduce a focus on critical listening following procedures like those Jo Hall used for writing analysis (Chapter Seven, pp. 97–101). Material may come from outside the class as well as from within it. Initial discussion can focus on:

- who the intended audience appeared to be;
- how one determined the likely audience;
- what the speakers' intentions appeared to be; and
- how the intentions were indicated.

Later analyses can look more closely at the aspects of language that writing analysis involves including such things as technique, logic and vocabulary.

That the teacher begins with 'showing how you respond' and then moves gradually towards the students learning to respond more analytically is important because the most solid foundation for students beginning to learn about their own oral language is feedback about the effectiveness of what they are presently doing. Once they understand how they affect others, students will **themselves** see the need for improvement and will be less likely to resist changing. Then the emphasis can move more towards helping them set goals for improvement.

When students then work on specific goals, it can provide a sense of continuity in their work in oral English. Marion Burn got a year 9 class at Plympton High School to suggest their own learning goals and here is her report of how it went. It was a drama class, so although there was a focus on oral language, there was also an emphasis on how the students presented themselves in front of the rest of the class.

AN INDIVIDUALIZED APPROACH BASED ON STRENGTHS AND GOALS

'Okay. Today I want you to prepare the worst play you can imagine.'

Silent disbelief. Then a few giggles. A barrage of questions. I reassured them that it was okay today to be absolute, utter failures. In fact, I wanted them to take the task seriously so that they presented as many well-considered mistakes as possible.

They embraced the idea with enthusiasm and delight. Some thought they would come on stage and just do nothing. I encouraged them to give more specific indications of their ideas of a play that doesn't work.

'Think of a good play first. What makes it a good play?'

You don't have more than one thing going on at once and you remember who you are.'

'Great. So, now reverse those ideas and show me what it would look like.'

Four groups presented brilliantly mis-shapen, uncoordinated slap-stick dramas which had us in fits. After each one we listed the aspects about it which made it so terribly bad. They were very articulate and delighted in pulling each one to pieces. (Like teachers, they are very practised at this.) The presenting groups took time to adjust to the onslaught of criticism and sometimes defended their actions:

'But it was meant to be like that! We planned that bit to go wrong.'

It was important for me to remind them of the original intention and help them to see that criticism in this case was praise.

Others felt a bit embarrassed that unintentional mistakes were being lauded.

I wrote the lists on butcher's paper, encouraging them to make their criticisms more specific, or giving them new terms to express their point:

'Well, Peter kept telling Barry it was his turn to speak, and that wasn't supposed to be in the play.'

'So, Peter didn't stay in his role. He played the burglar in the play and also played Peter, himself. We'll call this "not staying in role".'

The final list was very comprehensive and detailed.

> *e.g. It all happened too quickly.*
> *They didn't face the audience.*
> *They couldn't be heard.*
> *The characters didn't develop.*
> *Uncoordinated — they didn't watch each other.*
> *Didn't stay in role.*
> *They forgot their parts.*
> *The props were in the wrong places.*
> *No spontaneous improvisation.*
> *Giggling, laughing, fidgeting.*
> *Clumsy.*
> *It was boring — it had no clear plot.*

It was an exhilarating, cohesive lesson.

The next day my aim was to get them to articulate a list of skills to aim for. The list of mistakes was used as a resource and I had asked them to list skills in four categories:

> *Individual*
> *In Group Work*
> *An Audience*
> *Play Structure*

I explained that the skills were to cover all aspects of our lessons, not just the performances or presentations. So, for example, they were to think of what skills a group needed when preparing a play together. I introduced the idea of audience skills by asking:

> *Consider what kinds of audience responses are most helpful to you when you are presenting something. What do you most want from your audience that will encourage you to present and will enable you to know more about how you presented?*

I split the class into groups of 4 or 5, each with their own paper and pen, instructing them to choose a recorder and a spokesperson. The task was to write up all the skills they could think of under the four headings suggested, using the list of mistakes from yesterday's lesson to give them ideas. Again I was impressed by the breadth of their awareness. I prompted groups to consider aspects they had overlooked:

I see you've got 'stay in role'. What happens if someone tries to stay in role and someone else does something that wasn't planned? What skill do you need then?

and

You've written that you want positive comments from the audience. Well, sometimes I'll be asking the audience to point out parts that didn't work. What do you want from them then?

After fifteen minutes the groups came together and each spokesperson read out the group's list, explaining any confusions and answering questions. The list of audience skills warmed up the audience to their role to the extent that they hammed it up, indicating just how clearly they grasped these expectations!

After the lesson, I summarized their lists, and drew up posters to pin up in the drama room. Here are the lists of skills they suggested.

Individual
1) Voice — loud and clear.
2) Stay in role, concentrate (don't fidget, laugh or overact).
3) Face the audience.
4) Improvise — be spontaneous.
5) Take a risk by trying something new.
6) Remember your part.

In Group Work
1) Co-operate (share ideas, listen to each other, include everyone).
2) Concentrate (don't laugh at each other).
3) Co-ordinate (don't all speak at once, focus on one action at a time).
4) Persevere — work through problems.
5) Organize props, costumes.

As Audience
1) Give constructive feedback.
2) Applause.
3) Pay attention by looking, keeping quiet, laughing at the right time.

Play Structure
1) Rehearse.
2) Build up to the main part.
3) Include sufficient detail.
4) Timing — don't rush.

The outcomes for me up to this point were quite significant. I realized that the class was aware of many of the aims in drama and was able to demonstrate this in a very concrete way. I was clearer about my aims too, and we now had a common reference point. We shared clear information about criteria I could use for assessing their skills.

So far, this had been an exercise focused on the group as a whole. Now I wanted to assess the strengths of each student according to the criteria we had set, and help them set their own personal goals.

The next stage of the procedure was to observe and record their individual strengths and goals. I drew up a form which I called 'Drama Achievement Record', and divided the page into two under the headings 'Strengths' and 'Goals'. I informed the class that I intended to observe each of them in class and write up a list of their strengths. I soon found it was impossible to conduct even the most inactive lessons and compile these lists at the same time. However, I discovered that outside of the class room situation I could recall students' recent performances or behaviour well enough to confidently list strengths they displayed. I used the skills we had compiled in class, but I did not restrict myself to them.

When I handed the class their Achievement Records, I stressed that the list of strengths for each person wasn't necessarily comprehensive, and that the records would be used to help me assess their progress and for them to become aware of their own strengths and goals. They were very curious and impressed by the forms. They wanted to know what strengths each other had, and shared their records with others. Some terms needed explaining, and I reminded some students of recent occasions when I had observed them demonstrating their strengths.

After giving them time for discussion, I set them the task of setting three goals for themselves, by using the lists of skills as a guide and by recalling their past performances and the kind of feedback they had received. They took the task seriously and all wrote very appropriate goals. Some students needed to focus on a recent activity in order to define their goal in specific terms.

Some examples of individual goals set:

- *don't giggle;*
- *don't turn my back to the audience;*
- *attend lessons more regularly;*
- *act naturally in the role that I'm playing;*
- *try not to develop only comedy scenes.*

After collecting the records, I explained that during the following week we would refer to their goals, and once they had successfully mastered each one, these would be transferred to their list of strengths, and new goals would be set.

Gradually the procedure was becoming more personalized and hopefully more relevant for each student. I now wanted to use the goals each student had set to direct them specifically in improving their performance in Drama.

The class was familiar with spontaneous improvisation, and I chose this work for their first attempt to achieve one of the goals they had set themselves. Before the improvisation, someone would volunteer to begin. I would ask them to name one of the goals they had listed so that the audience could then give specific feedback on this goal when the improvisation had finished.

The improvisations would always involve other students, who would enter the scene at various times. These people would also get feedback from the audience, but the main focus was always on whoever had begun the scene. Invariably, there was a marked improvement in this student's performance. Identifying the goal beforehand enabled her to concentrate on the goal specifically, and the immediacy of the feedback helped her to relate this to her own experience.

Another significant change I observed was in the quality of the audience's responses. The class was more articulate and specific in their feedback, showing a greater awareness of the range of skills demonstrated, and more observant in their assessment of each other.

One student who made outstanding progress in this single activity was a girl called Fiona. Her greatest problem was self-consciousness which caused her to giggle inappropriately. In one scene she took the part of a company manager, faced with financial problems and complaints from clients. Confronted with these difficulties, she played a believable, serious role, responding imaginatively and spontaneously throughout.

A few weeks before I began this scheme, I had taken some movie film of the class doing some mimed plays, set to the Pink Panther music.

The films had just been developed and the class was very excited about seeing themselves on screen. I decided that this would be very appropriate time for them to check out their list of strengths and goals against their performance on film. Although the work on film had preceeded this compilation of strengths and goals, I suggested to them to watch out for any other strengths which they could add to the list, or likewise, any goals.

I made this suggestion before we viewed the films for the third time, and received a lot of groans and complaints, in particular from the boys. I was feeling ill with the flu during this lesson, and decided not to spend any precious energy dealing with this negative reaction, and pushed on with the task regardless.

Expecting the worst, I was in fact surprised by the seriousness with which many kids, mainly the girls, had accepted the task. They had made some perceptive observations, adding new strengths to their lists. Nevertheless, I was worried by the negative reaction from the others.

Despite its mixed success on this occasion, I believe this could be a very useful strategy, helping kids to identify their own strengths and goals. The impact of seeing oneself is very powerful. It is unbiased, concrete feedback which allows the viewer to distance herself from her involvement in the performance and see her actions from the point of view of the audience.

The next week I introduced another task involving strengths and goals, and again was greeted with groans from the boys, so I set the task aside and spent time with them reviewing and exploring their feelings about this work.

The main complaints were that they hated paper work and resented any time which detracted from the time available for work on their presentations. When asked whether they had benefited at all from identifying their strengths and *goals, the majority agreed they had, and could specify times when it had helped them. They had simply had enough of it. After listening to, and clarifying their reactions, I proposed that today's activity would be the last one for some time where they had to do any writing, and that although we would be referring to their goals in future, I would not take any substantial time away from their presentations. They were happy with this arrangement, so I introduced the task I had prepared.*

The aim of this task was to encourage them to reflect on their own progress in terms of the goals they had set, and to specify times when they had worked on particular goals. I informed them that I would take into account what they wrote when writing comments for their report cards. If they could give clear evidence of working towards a goal, then I would be better able to judge their level of achievement. I stressed that it was not always possible for me to observe everyone's progress in terms of specific goals, so this could add to the information I already had.

The task was taken very seriously and no one had any trouble remembering times when they had worked towards a goal. Without exception, I agreed with all the comments. I found the report writing much easier and more relevant than ever before. I was able to mention many of the goals they achieved in their reports, often using the same expressions they had written. My comments were more specific and non-judgemental, and I felt more in touch with the progress of each individual.

I am sure there are many variations on this idea of working with strengths and goals. Some of my plans for future lessons are:

- *to assess the strengths and goals of some of their favourite TV stars, and to discuss these together;*

- *to choose someone else in the class to give feedback on a specific aspect of performance;*

- *to design activities which challenge students to work towards a goal many of the class share;*

- *to write their own reports in a more comprehensive way than I have done so far.*

I believe there is much to recommend this scheme. Most important perhaps, are the self-assessment skills which the kids learn along the way. Rather than viewing themselves as being either good or bad at drama, or even good or bad per se, this strategy allows them to see themselves as possessing strengths in some areas, even if their overall performance is poor. It gives them clear, specific information about what they can do and a language to articulate what they could aim for next.

This kind of assessment focuses on the positive rather than what is lacking. Its basic implication is that everyone can progress and although high standards are aimed for, the learning is personal rather than competitive. Its language is non-judgemental and activity-related, thus avoiding a static, definitive stance.

For my job, this kind of procedure gives me a wealth of useful, relevant information about my class. I can communicate with them what I know about their skills and what I think they should aim for. My criteria for assessment are no longer hidden, and I feel less worried about giving negative feedback because it is related to specific goals, rather than being seen as a judgement of the person.

The procedure can be ongoing, which provides a view of drama as developmental rather than a series of unrelated activities. The status of the subject is also enhanced by the visibility of a curriculum, a set of skills which communicates an overall design to the course.

To summarize, this approach can be applied to oral English by, firstly, having the students prepare and present demonstrations of ineffective oral language. This is best done in groups. At the end of each presentation, the class identifies the ineffective features and these are listed on a chart. Some time later, the class, again in groups, devises a list of positive qualities using the lists of ineffective features as a stimulus. Then the students identify their goals for development, drawing on the list of positive qualities for ideas. They are reminded of their goals during subsequent class work and given specific feedback in relation to them.

In oral English, there would usually be more emphasis on goals which involved the speakers achieving their purpose and structuring infor- mation appropriately, than applied in Marion's drama class.

This approach works best when the focus is on oral language in a particular, defined situation, for example, speaking to an unknown adult, to a whole class or in a working group.

The students' commitment to the learning can be expected to be stronger if they choose the situation they will concentrate on — and within the one class there can be students working on different situations. Then students learn both from what their group does — and from observing and responding when other groups present their examples of poor performance, list their criteria and set goals in relation to the situations they chose to work on.

In this book, I have presented three examples where teachers helped their students to articulate criteria for assessing their work in English and where the criteria came from the students' own experience. One example was Marion's work in drama; another, Steve Dowdy's work on experimenting in writing reported in Chapter Four; and the third, Jo Hall's work which leads to the students' self-assessment (Chapter Seven). Once they have experienced these activities, students under- stand the notion of setting their own learning goals — and they are better placed to evaluate goals which the teacher may set for them, because they can compare them with the goals they set themselves.

This is the last chapter which focuses directly on how teachers can take a student-centred approach to helping students reflect on their own and their peers' language. The next chapters turn to judgemental assessment. In Chapters Ten and Eleven, I discuss how judgemental assessment can be organized so as to minimize its interference with student reflection. Then, in Chapter Twelve, I discuss how teachers help students to clarify the demands of judgemental assessment. Finally Chapter Thirteen addresses the related concerns of reporting and state-wide examining.

10 Organizing Judgemental Assessment I: Work-Required Assessment

In most schools there is a requirement that the quality of students' work be judged. Judgement should be organized so that it does not pervade all of classroom life, for when it does it discourages reflection and experimentation, in fact learning itself. But the process of learning is not the whole story. A sense of progress towards institutionally recognized goals — or towards an excellent product — is also important.

Peter Elbow wrote 'In Piaget's terms learning involves both assimilation and accommodation. Part of the job is to get the subject matter to bend and deform so that it fits inside the learner (that is, so it can fit or relate to the learner's experiences). But that's only half the job. Just as important is the necessity for the learner to bend and deform himself so that he can fit himself around the subject without doing violence to it.'[1]

This chapter describes how teachers can set up an arena of judgement which students approach, knowing it is time for them to put their best foot forward. The focus of the judgements is the focus of English, language use, not general descriptions of behaviour or personality. Assessment should be a clear-cut matter of reporting whether the student has been engaged in the specified requirements of the course, and where they are required, judgements of the quality of the student's work.

In these academic assessments, judgemental terms like 'excellent' and 'unsatisfactory' should be avoided because they imply that some students should gain approval and some disapproval. We know that some progress more quickly than others, but this is no reason to grant them more approval. We can keep the language of assessment closer to an accurate description of the students' achievements than that. 'Excellent' for example, when used on reports is often an irresponsible and very loose use of language, offered more as an emotional reward than an articulate description.

I will discuss two approaches to organizing judgemental assessment. In this chapter I describe work-required assessment. In the next I discuss the more usual practice of emphasizing judgements based on comparisons between students.

Much that is important in a course need not lead to formal judgement of the quality of students' products. Where teachers have confidence that certain processes will provide powerful learning experiences, they can specify that the student must be involved in them to be considered successful. This can be a very demanding requirement indeed. For example, work-required assessed courses in South Australia and Victoria often require that students prepare written work by drafting, editing, reading it to another age group, reflecting on the reading and audience reaction, rewriting, polishing and publication. This is a more rigorous requirement than most students in traditional courses have ever imagined might be asked of them at school. Specifying the processes to be required gives teachers the opportunity to apply the concept of rigour to the demands they make. This contrasts with traditional education where rigour may refer to an ideal in an assessor's head, but nothing more.[2]

This approach to assessment is referred to as work-required assessment. It was first developed in Victorian secondary schools in the late 1970s,[3] when it was referred to as goal-based assessment. Now, in both Victoria and South Australia, whole schools use this approach in all subject areas and there are year 12 accredited subjects based on it. Initially the promotion of work-required assessment emphasized that it is non-competitive. Now that it is more widespread the emphasis is more on how effective it can be in involving the range of students in productive work.

A CONTRACT BETWEEN TEACHER AND STUDENT

Work-required assessment operates from some very down-to-earth assumptions about schooling, namely that students are at school to work and learn and that the teacher's job is to offer them activities through which they will learn.

In work-required assessment, the teacher offers students a contract of the form, if you are involved in the processes which make up this course, then you'll learn and the school will recognize this by reporting that you have successfully completed the course. If you don't involve yourself in these processes then we won't say you've completed the course. In most cases it is clearly stated in the student's report if the course has not been completed (NC). Most students hate to get an NC. They are much more accountable to their parents for an NC (because they can be asked 'Why didn't you complete that particular work?'), than they are for a low grade like a D where they can make excuses by blaming the teacher ('She gave me a D!') or putting themselves down ('I'm just not good at English').

The advantage of work-required assessment is that the students need not waste time and energy being anxious about being judged successful or unsuccessful on unknown criteria. they still get anxious about particular requirements of a course, but they can channel their energy specifically towards facing that requirement, leading to more productive learning than is common in anxiety-ridden, traditional schooling.

Under this approach, the teacher has a coaching role, which is to remind the students that they are to be fully involved in the processes. Jo Hall reports that in first term:

> I have to remind students that they have to be fully involved, 'not with your mind three-quarters somewhere else'. If they seem a bit distracted or to be just going through the motions I say that I think that's so. That irritates them sometimes, but in this course that is the assessment. They have to be concentrating on the activities.
>
> The standards are built into the course. Much of their writing is read to younger kids, which is very demanding. And teacher and student both have to be satisfied that each process has been fully gone through.

So the coaching role is also a teaching role in that it encourages the students to take the responsibility to reflect and learn.

STANDARDS

The teacher also negotiates the standard of work which will be accepted as indicating successful engagement in an activity. It is not a case of anything is good enough. Early in the course, the teacher discusses with the class how the purpose of each requirement suggests what will constitute completed work. For example, if a journal is to be kept, a certain purpose will need to have been achieved. The journal may need to demonstrate that the student is experimenting with different styles and forms of writing. Or it may need to show development in the student's ability to produce a traditional 'lit crit' essay (the development may be from a first draft to a later, more accomplished draft which takes teacher suggestions into account, or, it may be shown over a series of pieces during a term). Alternatively, the purpose of a journal may be simply to ensure that the student writes regularly, dates the writing and keeps it, in which case this must be achieved for successful completion.

Whatever the requirement is, teacher and students should have some common understanding of what its purpose is. Then work is endorsed as successfully completed when both student and teacher are satisfied that the purpose has been achieved.

Of course, in most classrooms, the teacher is very much the more powerful party to this negotiation. Nevertheless, as Maurie Sheehan, a teacher at Hurstbridge High School, who has been using this approach for three years, explains, 'I'm the one who vets their work, but it's against criteria which the class has discussed early on. This gives them a sense of security and direction in their work'.

This attempt to make assessment a co-operative endeavour between teacher and student is at the heart of work-required assessment. It is not easy to describe this approach as if it is a formula to be followed, because teachers walk something of a tightrope, simultaneously emphasizing that the purpose of the work be achieved by all students, and adjusting their expectations of what is a good educational outcome depending on the individual student.

An example may help make this clearer. A year 10 work-required course included the requirement that students 'for both novel and play, write a substantial piece which accurately reflects the world of the text: discuss this with peers and revise where appropriate.' The students had read Colin Thiele's *Blue Fin* and, at the teacher's suggestion, some decided to write an extra chapter describing the clipper, *Dog Star*'s, disappearance, which is left to the reader's imagination in Thiele's novel.

Discussion between teacher and students generates further clarification of what a student must do to complete this task. For example, it might well be expected that:

- the incident be described in a measure of detail which matches the style of the original novel;

- there be no glaring incompatibilities in content or style between the extra chapter and the original novel;

- there be no long irrelevant sections which distract the reader from the focus of the chapter;

- the writing be clear as to what is meant.

Clearly these are not objective criteria, like those which criterion-referenced assessment uses, but they are valuable nevertheless. In work-required assessment a teacher may say to a student 'in all honesty I can't report successful completion of this task because I don't think you've given enough detail'. The teacher's job is then to help the student write in more relevant detail. The judgement as to when it is detailed enough will be subjective and a point of valuable discussion between teacher and student. It is the disucssion of these subjective judgements which is a crucial element in good teaching, and work-required assessment highlights the importance of such discussion, because students are given time to rework assignments which are judged not successful.

A further element of subjectivity is introduced because, in a creative subject like English, different students choose work at very different levels of ambition. A student who has a particular talent will find the teacher expecting her to extend herself further in that area, while accepting less from a student who has a lot of difficulties. This leaves a lot to the discretion of the teacher. The teacher's intuitive sense of when to expect more and when to be satisfied an educationally worthwhile outcome has been achieved and should be credited, is at the heart of teaching regardless of the assessment method used. However work-required assessment encourages teachers to back their judgements of students, rather than letting many talented students simple coast along. Talented students are required to experiment in new ways, revise their work, and work on goals for improvement just the same as everyone else.

Students accept that different standards are expected of different students' products, as long as it is explained at the beginning of the course that this is how things will go — that all are expected to show persistence in developing their work through involvement in learning activities. The standard required is involvement and extension in the processes stipulated. From the students' point of view, it is a fair and achievable expectation. From the teacher's point of view, it is important that the work required of students is a documentation of how all the students are being challenged to learn.

TEACHERS AND STUDENTS AS ALLIES

If students are fully involved in the required processes, but they do not learn, that this is a sign that the course needs to be reconsidered and more powerful processes used. These courses work best when the requirements are decided by a group of teachers, for example, the English department within a school, and documented for all to see. Apart from the advantage of drawing on the experience of a number of teachers rather than just one, the 'department agreed' set of requirements will not seem like an obstacle erected at the arbitrary whim of the class teacher. Peter Elbow highlights the advantages of clearly documented requirements:

> Documents heighten the sense that I do indeed take responsibility for these standards; writing them forces me to try to make them as concrete, explicit and objective as possible (if not necessarily fair). But most of all having put all this on paper I can more easily go on to separate myself from them in some way — leave them standing — and turn around and schizophrenically start being a complete ally of the students.[4]

Work-required assessment is intended to bring about a situation in which most students are successful and know what it is they have succeeded in doing. Failure is reserved, in the main, for those who lack the determination to meet all the demands. So students who are not successful know what it is that they have not done and will usually have chosen not to persevere.

When rigorous demands are made, some students find it difficult to meet them, but with the teacher's help most who show persistence succeed. Thus the emphasis is very squarely on the teacher–student partnership. **With the teacher's help**, some students will achieve beyond the level they would reach on their own. It is easy to see that as a cause for error in the assessments: the way we have traditionally thought about assessment has assumed that students should be assessed on what they can do **on their own** — as if they exist as isolated individuals. Traditionally, we have taken that to be a more valid test than asessing how students work when help is available and when they must show persistence and responsibility to get and act on the help. But if we want our education system to equip students to work in this more social way, then we should change our assumptions about what is valid assessment procedure. We should allow personal interactions to contribute to the work which is assessed.

(This is how schools' assessment processes can foster students' interpersonal effectiveness. We should not formally assess interpersonal behaviour at school, because it is so dependent on the context in which the interactions take place.)

WORK-REQUIRED ASSESSMENT IN PRACTICE

Work-required assessment can be a good or a bad system. Mostly it depends on the work required. If students are simply presented with a list of products they must submit, there is no guarantee that they will learn, their motivation is likely to be low and the teacher will have problems with some students completing the course while others are not yet half-way through.

Work-required assessment is better when the emphasis is more on defining ongoing **processes** that lead to learning in the particular subject area, and expressing the requirements in such a way that they are specific enough to give students appropriate expectations of what they'll be doing, but broad enough that students will have freedom to make decisions about how and when they will work on the requirements.

This point is taken up in the case study of work-required assessment to be presented now. This study has been prepared by Steve Dowdy of Ingle Farm High School. His initial 'Contracts' (lists of work required) were substantially lists of products, but more recently they emphasize how students learn.

The report form included (opposite), lists the work required on the

English

| Term | 198 |
| Year level | 10 |

Name   **C.G.**

To complete this course, students had to:-

<u>WRITTEN LANGUAGE</u>:

(1) Keep a folder of Silent Sustained Writing and whole class writing activities.   ___

(2) Show evidence of re-drafting and experimentation and select one polished piece for assessment each month.   ___

(3) Produce a written response to the mysteries read.   ___

(4) Keep a Writing Process card up to date.   ___

<u>LITERATURE</u>:

(1) Read a set novel and complete a negotiated response.   ___

(2) Read independently and widely.   ___

(3) Complete a Recommendation Card, a negotiated written response or present an oral report on all independent reading.   ___

<u>ORAL LANGUAGE</u>:

In addition to informal oral work:

(1) Present a researched topic to the class.   ___

(2) Maintain an Oral Work Record Card.   ___

<u>POETRY</u>:

(1) Read a variety of poems.   ___

(2) Negotiate a response to the poetry read.   ___

<u>COMPUTING</u>:

Use the computer network for text editing and adventure game activity.   ___

<u>ADDITIONAL WORK</u>:

Subject Teacher ————

S.Dowdy

left hand side. Work is coded as 'S' (successfully completed), 'NC' (not successfully completed) and where a specific product is called for, there is a third category, 'NS' (task completed, but product has not yet satisfied demands discussed in class). This 'NS' category is an innovation of Steve's, not a usual feature in work-required assesment. It does serve to reinforce in parents' minds that standards are spelt out and insisted upon. As you read his study you will find that Steve also tried an extra category, 'M', for a product which is 'worthy of being used as a model for other students of this year level'. This 'M' category represented a compromise between work-required assessment and the traditional grading based on comparisons between students and Steve evaluates its usefulness in his case study.

WORK-REQUIRED ASSESSMENT IN YEAR 11 ENGLISH AT INGLE FARM HIGH SCHOOL

Introducing the contract

At the beginning of Term One I presented students with a contract of work which I had organised. Students were also given a letter to take home which explained the philosophy and method of operation of the system and which contained an invitation for parents to contact me at any time throughout the year to clarify issues (see letter opposite).

After distributing a typed copy of the initial contract to each student and allowing time for reading and informal discussion, I began to explain why I had organized the term's course in the way I had, what my role would be and what I hoped they would achieve.

I pointed out that the contract was an offer of work, that we would negotiate whole class and individual aspects throughout the term and that there would be progressively more scope for negotiation and variation as the year progressed. Discussion followed in response to students' questions and by the end of the week most students were comfortable with the concept. Most were reassured by the existence of a contract of work, and the more independent learners recognised that they would have some control over what they would do in certain facets of the course.

Allowing scope for negotiation became more important as the year progressed when students began to offer suggestions about activities which they felt would develop their English. These suggestions were discussed in class and a collective decision was made, whether the activities would be included as a non-negotiable component of the programme of work. Contracts were not fixed, teacher directed, constricting documents. Three weeks before the end of term, we formulated the final draft of the contract which was typed and presented in the form of a report sheet.

Only one student was opposed to trialling the system. Fiona spoke volubly against it. She believed my job was to teach grammar, set exercises and then

INGLE FARM HIGH SCHOOL

Belalie Road Ingle Farm   S.A. 5098   Telephone 2602022
Principal: M.S. Reynolds, B.A. Dip Ed., Dip. Phys. Ed., Dip. T. M.A.C.E.

26th February 1984.

Dear Parent(s)/Guardian,

I am writing to let you know that   's year 11 report will be organised differently than the reports you have received in previous years.

The report you will receive will be set out like the sheet attached to this letter. It will tell you
- what work has been required in the course
- whether your child has completed the set work successfully
- and any areas that need further attention
- where appropriate I will write comments on the right hand side of the form to indicate what needs to be done or what extra help I might offer

The report will also indicate if any particular piece of work has been done so well that it could be used as an example for other students to learn from.

This new approach to reporting is being introduced in a number of schools in South Australia and Victoria. The major advantage of the new approach is that students can understand more precisely what they are expected to acheive in English. To success-fully complete the course, students will need to gain an 'S' (for successful) alongside each requirement. I will let the students know in class what standard their work must reach to be considered successful and they will be free to seek help from me and their class mates. As well they will be able to do the work again if their first efforts are not successful.

I hope that the new reports also let you know more about what English involves. If you don't understand some of what you read in the report, please ask your child about it. If, after that, you still do not understand, or if you wish to discuss the course content or reporting procedure with me, don't hesitate to contact me at the school (phone 260.2022).

As in previous years, the 'School-Leaver's Statement' will continue to be the report form meant for employers. However, some employers insist on seeing the reports addressed to parents. While the new approach is not designed for employers, it will provide them with a more informative description of the student's achieve-ments than has previously been available.

During the year I will be asking some parents to comment on the new report forms. I would very much appreciate hearing any reactions you might have.

M.S. Reynolds
Principal

Yours faithfully

Stephen Dowdy
English Senior

mark tests to check that the exercises had been done and the grammar understood. When interviewed by Brian Johnston in August, Fiona's views had changed little, despite recognizing that she had been involved in a greater variety of more demanding learning exercises than in previous years.

> Fiona: *I've worked harder than in previous years because you have to redo work to get it right. I've read more and written in different ways but not all of this has been marked and we haven't had enough grammar tests. I hate having to do oral work too.*

Refining contracts

My initial contract was far too product orientated. For instance, I stipulated titles of texts and the number of written pieces to be presented for assessment. I understood the philosophy inherent in work-required assessment but I was not able to translate it into the terms of a contract. I now construct contracts which define broad learning processes. Such contracts enable students to negotiate activities and products which are personally challenging and achievable.

For instance, in my initial contract the study of literature section stipulated that students were expected to:–

1)   *Read 2 class novels and discuss incidents, characters and their personal reactions.*   _____

2)   *Keep a reading journal in which they explore their response to the novels in writing.*   _____

3)   *Present a polished piece on each text*
     ● The Outsiders
     ● The Great Gilly Hopkins   _____

4)   *Wider reading: Read three books of their own choice. Present an oral summary of two and a written response to the other.*   _____

While this format included processes such as reading, discussing, reflecting, polishing, publishing and explaining, doubts as to its effectiveness were raised by Tracy who objected to reading The Great Gilly Hopkins. *The dialogue between Tracy and me regarding her reluctance to read went like this:*

> Dowdy: *Tracy, I've noticed that you haven't finished reading* Gilly Hopkins.

> Tracy: *Yeah and I don't want to, it's boring.*

> Dowdy: *But you have to, it's part of the contract. Now that we've agreed to it and the rest of the class is reading it I'll have no options but to record NC against it on your assessment and I don't want to do that. You know that these records are transferred into the report sheet.*

> Tracy: *I don't care and not everyone is readng it anyway. Paul isn't.*

> Dowdy: *Well, I'll take that up with Paul but if you don't want to read the book then you've made a choice about your assessment sheet. Think about it.*

I don't know whether Tracy thought about it but I did. A couple of days later, I went back to Tracy and I tried again.

> Dowdy: *Tracy, will you please explain why you don't want to read* Gilly Hopkins*?*

> Tracy: *Well, I started it and it was boring. I read about forty pages and it didn't interest me so I don't want to continue reading it. I don't like books like that. I'm willing to read, but not that book.*

With the last sentence it became clear to me. By having a watertight contract stipulating titles, I wasn't giving students choice. I asked myself whether I valued The Great Gilly Hopkins *or whether I valued reading, sharing, reflecting, clarifying and students connecting that experience to the world of the novel. The answer was clear and I now write contracts like this:*

To complete the course students were expected to:
1) *Read a novel and complete a negotiated response to be presented to an appropriate audience.*   _____

2) *Develop and fulfil a personal reading contract which will include*

   - *keeping a record of all reading.*

   - *extending the types of books read.*

   - *reading at home and at school.*

   - *sharing reading with a member of the class.*   _____

I now suggest titles for reading and in most cases students have the choice whether to accept the offering or to pick another title in negotiation with me as Tracy did. The result is I now work more frequently with small groups on individual tasks than teach the whole class in a lock step manner. Nevertheless, when there is a need, I still have teacher directed lessons. If, for instance, there are issues emanating from a novel which a large group is studying, those who are reading another text, or who are engaged in another contracted activity may either stay in the classroom and be involved in the lesson because it is of interest or they negotiate to work in another area of the English building or in the Resource Centre.

Challenge for all

Work-required assessment is based on the philosophy of ensuring success is achievable for all students and therefore contracts must be written in a way which allows negotiation of challenging activities for all students. Unless this happens contracts can often degenerate to become a list of products which means that some students are not being challenged while others have no realistic hope of success.

For instance, if all students are expected to produce the same product, say a four page or 1500 word short story, in response to a contractual requirement such as: 'Experiment with new and different styles and forms of writing and polish one substantial piece of writing for inclusion in a class book', some students will have no hope of achieving success while others will not be challenged.

It is far better to negotiate what a substantial piece will be for each student. For a student who writes fluently and imaginatively a substantial product may be a short story which uses imagery and symbolism while a substantial product for a student who does not spell accurately and who has difficulty constructing sentences may be a one page story which is error free. If both students are being challenged they are extending the range of things they can do and therefore contractual requirements which follow can build upon success. For each, the demands become progressively more difficult.

Independent learning

Trialling this assessment procedure forced me to re-evaluate a number of my practices as students became more articulate in seeking information about the purpose for each activity. They soon learned that in discussions about the contract we would try to establish the criteria for assessment of each separate activity. In each case, students needed to know the purpose and audience. It soon became the practice that students were involved in defining the criteria for assessment of each separate activity. They, as well as I, had the raw data to decide whether their work had been successfully completed.

For example, a number of students worked to deliver a speech to the class. Even though the topics varied, we agreed an effective presentation would result from students looking at the audience, adopting an appropriate stance and considering the effect of body language, speaking in a voice which is clear and audible, variation in tone and pace, using expressive language, imagery, gestures and aids, linking ideas, rehearsing, seeking feedback and reflecting upon advice given.

Once they had this information my role was seen in a different light. In response to students' requests, I spent time pointing out aspects of work which I believed did not meet the quality required by the agreed criteria. This was seen as constructive advice rather than summary judgement. Students spent a good deal of time checking my perceptions against those of other class members.

An atmosphere of co-operative endeavour began to develop; the students and I were working together to meet the demands imposed by the contract: an external thing.

This system forced me to be more articulate about what students needed to do to achieve success and the students became more knowledgeable about what they were doing and the learning purpose of each activity. As they were involved in developing the criteria for assessment of each activity they were able to evaluate their own performance.

The nature of the assessment

The following coding was used in response to each piece of work required:

S: *Successfully completed.*

M: *Successfully completed product, worthy of being used as a model for other students of this year level.*

NS: *Task completed, but product doesn't satisfy all the defined demands of the task.*

NC: *Task not completed.*

There was no attempt to combine the responses into an overall grade because work-required assessment tries to paint an accurate and detailed picture of each individual's strengths and areas requiring improvement. The code 'S' indicates whether the defined demands were met, and comments either identify areas of excellence or provide diagnostic advice for improvement of the student's performance.

Because there is no averaging of performance over a number of different areas this system places more stringent demands on students. All aspects of the course are recognised as being important, and for a course to be successfully completed requires a quality response to each requirement. Some students felt this was unfair. For instance, Simone questioned the necessity for involvement in oral work:

Simone: *Look, I've never talked in front of the class because I'm not good at it and I don't like it. It's never stopped me from passing before and I don't see why we can't just forget that part.*

Dowdy: *Simone, you said you weren't good at talking in front of a group. Can you tell me what it is that you're not good at?*

Simone: *It's not so much that I'm not good at it, I suppose I could do it but I don't want to.*

Dowdy: *Unfortunately this method of operation doesn't allow that as a choice. We agreed, as a class, that reading, writing and oral work were non-negotiable. Your choice is not whether you do it but what you do. My job is to help you work out something which can be practised and which will show you that you can be good at talking in front of people.*

Simone took up this challenge and we spent time working on a speech. It is at this stage when working on a specific challenge that most teaching and learning occurs. After a number of rehearsals in front of progressively larger groups, Simone's report for the oral language section read:

1) Prepare a formal speech on a topic of their choice, and receive feedback.   _S_

Simone asked for advice from me and other members of the class on ways of varying the tone of her voice. She acted upon the responses given and her presentation to the class was fluent, confident and entertaining. The use of a live 'sleepy lizard' was a very effective way of getting the attention of the class. A great effort!

This method of response is more informative than the traditional form of grading because it not only acknowledges success in response to defined demands for which there are agreed criteria, but it also details aspects of the work which ensure success. Similarly, if some components of the course have not been completed, or if the quality of response is poor, this will be identified. For example, Mark's report for the Writing Workshop section indicated the following:

- With other students develop a list of aspects of quality writing and provide examples.   _M_

  Articulate and involved in whole class discussion. Provided a comprehensive range of effective criteria and selected examples which illustrated these.

- Keep a sustained writing folder   _S_

  Experimented with a number of different styles of writing and shared some of these with the class.

- Work in a responding and editing group.   _M_

  Great help to others. Was constructive in offering ideas for improving the quality of work.

- Present for assessment four polished pieces which show evidence of redrafting and experimentation.   _NC_

  Only first drafts submitted. Although writing presented was error free, no attempt was made to expand the range of writing with which he is familiar. He must experiment and take risks in written work.

A far clearer picture of Mark's ability to write is developed than could occur if all of these aspects, and often other skill areas, are aggregated and averaged into a single grade. The clarity of the report was illustrated by Mario's response when he saw his report at the end of Term One. Although he had access to the record-keeping book throughout the term, and therefore the information of the report, he was shocked at NC being recorded against most of the defined demands. He stammered, 'Don't give me that, it shows too much. I want a U' (the bottom grade). Aftr a period of discussion he acknowledged that while he had commenced many activities he had not completed them to the stage where they satisfied the agreed criteria. Throughout the term, Mario had agreed that his work needed refinement. However he had not refined the work and saw the consequence of his lack of commitment.

Dean's report had a number of NC codes recorded and comments indicated that he had shown competence in a number of areas but he had not polished work. I found his initial reaction interesting. He said 'At least NC shows that I didn't do it, not that I couldn't'. Mario then asked him 'Yeah, well how are you going to explain that to your parents? I bet they will ask why you didn't finish the work'. The Term Two Parent/Teacher night confirmed Mario's prediction. However, Dean's parents were particularly pleased with the detail and clarity of the report. They said their discussions with Dean had been far more beneficial then previous considerations of reports because they could identify aspects of the course and ask about them. As a result, Dean's application and work quality improved. As he gained success, his confidence grew and gradually he began to work more independently.

Further information on the coding system was sought by Brian Johnston when he interviewed some students:

Marie: *The new procedure gives a better outline of what you've been good at — and not good at. (She gave her own examples): Usually you get a U for not finishing. Here it says NC which is more accurate.*

Robert: *This looks good. The others, they don't write about your English just your attitude. Your English is what the reports should be about!*

Brian: *Isn't this a sign of standards dropping? As long as you do it you get an S?*

Paul: *No, if you're just doing the minimum you'd get an NS. It's completed but not that good. This is better because you know what you've done and you can continue to redraft it until you get an S.*

This system ensures that learning becomes a self-conscious activity. Students become aware of their strengths and weaknesses and recognize that a good try is not necessarily a successfully completed product. Often a fair attempt would have been awarded a C or D, whichever is the lowest passing grade. In comparison, there is no S−, by definition this becomes NS.

This system ensures that learning becomes a self-conscious activity. Students become aware of their strengths and weaknesses and recognize that a good try is not necessarily a successfully completed product. Often a fair attempt would have been awarded a C or D, whichever is the lowest passing grade. In comparison, there is no S−, by definition this becomes NS.

A problem with the coding system became apparent. The category M was not achievable for all students but, more importantly, often it was not possible to explain to students what to do to achieve an M coding. On the one hand, I was working hard to establish an atmosphere where students took responsibility to clarify the demands of each task — and on the other hand I was undoing all that work by giving Ms on unexplained criteria. Students began to collect and covet Ms like they had As. Once a piece of work had M on it, students felt it became a model for all places and times.

Students who had worked effectively and learned new things were often gaining an S, but seeing this as comparative failure. At times I wasn't really sure whether I was awarding Ms for quality performance or, as is sometimes the case with As, as a reward for persistent endeavour. I believe that this weakened the system and now I use only the three categories — S, NS and NC. Excellence is identified in a descriptive comment. This makes it clear that the excellence being described is something which the marker has valued highly but it does not imply that this will remain an aspect of excellence if the nature of, or the purpose for the work changes.

High quality may also be rewarded by publication. Presenting speeches, displaying written material, compiling anthologies of work, and praising publicly are alternative and effective methods of motivating and rewarding students.

The result

Initially the progress of this trial was noted by members of the English faculty. As a result of student comment, other faculties also became interested in this method of assessment. In 1985 all members of the English faculty are using this method of assessment as a result of a faculty decision and other faculties are trialling work-required assessment.

THE INCOMPATIBILITY OF WORK-REQUIRED ASSESSMENT AND GRADES

Since 1984, work-required assessment has been used in South Australian schools, in all subject areas. In my experience, 80 per cent of the teachers who try it are enthusiastic. Parents appreciate the amount of comprehensible detail they get about their children's learning. When the contract of work-required allows students room to negotiate individual and group projects which are of interest to them, they too are enthusiastic.

Students and parents generally accept work-required assessment as a responsible approach to assessment in schools. At the same time, if they are asked if they would also like grades or marks, approximately 50 per cent indicate they would like these institutional rewards. They do not understand how traditional grading schemes contradict the basic elements of work-required assessment, namely its contractual basis and its co-operative approach to assessment.

Attempts to combine work-required assessment and grading are often made and they almost always mean that the advantages of work-required assessment are lost. This is a very important issue and I will now summarize why the two systems cannot be used together.

Attempts to combine work-required assessment and grades fit into two categories.

(1)   If students successfully complete the work required, then the products they come up with are graded.
(2)   Different contracts are specified in advance for the different grades.

If students successfully complete the work required, then the products they come up with are graded

There are three reasons why this is incompatible with work-required assessment.

Firstly, work-required assessment is particularly appropriate to courses in which students negotiate to develop their work in ways which are unpredictable and not standardised. This involves the students applying knowledge to situations of their own choosing. The work results in products which can not be validly compared. For example, in a year 8 science course, part of the work required for a unit on electricity was that students 'work in a small group to design and construct an electrical appliance and demonstrate it to the rest of the class' and that they 'keep a record of the project to show what you did and how you overcame problems'. All students had to develop their appliances to be more effective or complex than they were at first. The resulting products included an audio-amplifier, which worked, but had some unresolved problems, an electric drink dispenser, a very primitive whistling kettle which worked, and some conceptually simple, but elegantly presented matching games which used electrical connections. All students went through the defined learning processes to develop their work. They were therefore all successful. The students were working on such different tasks that to compare them using grades would be like asking whether Martina Navratilova is better than Alan Border. Any such comparisons would be idiosyncratic to the judge and would lack any general validity.

A second, but related, reason is that work-required assessment allows for, indeed at times sets up, glorious failures — very ambitious projects

which may end up with unresolved faults, but have involved consider-
able learning. Schools should offer environments where this type of
risk-taking and learning is safe, but when products are to be graded,
students who want to do well usually choose safe projects — which rely
on what they can already do well.

Thirdly, the teacher grading the students' products contradicts three
basic principles of work-required assessment, namely that the teacher
offers students a **contract** as to how they all can be successful learners;
that students **negotiate** to work in ways or on topics which concern
them; and that students and teacher are both **involved in assessing**
successful completion.

1) *Contract*: A contract should offer advantages to both parties. But
   if, for example, the grades A, B and C are awarded on the basis of
   the students' products, then C is a relative failure. Students who
   feel they are not likely to get an A or a B are unlikely to work hard
   for the dubious honour of a C; from their point of view the
   contract is a sham.

2) *Negotiation*: If two students negotiate with the teacher and then go
   on to successfully complete what they negotiated, and then one
   gets an A and the other a C, the one who gets the C would be
   justified in rejecting the negotiation proess — and the negotiating
   teacher! — because the teacher endorsed them working on
   something which was to give them a lesser result.

3) *Student involvement assessment*: If the teacher is making distinctions between satisfactory work (= C) and excellent work (= A)
   then it is the teacher's judgements which really count. Negotiated
   agreements about what completed means will be a sham and
   students will not be fooled by them.

Different contracts are specified for different grades.

At least this approach attempts to recognize that work-required
assessment gives students some responsibility to negotiate what they will
do. However the difficulties which arise in attempting to put this idea
into practice invalidate the distinctions made between the grades.

The contracts for the grades can differ in three ways:

1) *Contracts can differ in terms of the amount of work required*:
   Contracts should not simply require more work for an A than a B
   and so on. Grades are understood in our society (and many
   others) as indicators of quality. To use grades to report
   differences in amount of work, irrespective of quality, would be to
   mislead.

2) *All students' contracts may include core work, while some include extension work as well*: If the differentiations between grades are to be determined by giving a C for completing core work and a B or an A for completing supposedly more demanding extension work, students and teachers often move through the core work as if it is basic knowledge, hurrying on to develop their individual applications in the extension work. In contrast, the work-required approach is based on an assumption that all students will benefit from dwelling on and improving their performance on the learning processes which define the course. If high grades were to be earned through extension work, then requiring talented students to dwell on and develop core work would be directly handicapping them in the quest for a high grade.

3) *Contracts for higher grades may include more demanding or more complex learning processes than the contracts for lower or middle grades.* In most situations, the quality of the students' work cannot be predicted from a description of a supposedly more demanding learning process. For example, if students are expected to prepare a presentationfor the teacher, to get a C; for an audience of classmates, to get a B; and for a wider audience, to get an A, teachers would find that they had to give an A to a student who presented crude work to the wider audience; and a C to a student who presented elegant work only to the teacher. These grades would be misleading.

11 Organizing Judgemental Assessment II: Comparative Judgements Between Students

At present, many schools experience a heavy pressure to formally record comparative judgements between students, often in the form of grades or marks. What are teachers to do if they wish to implement assessment in ways which involve students in reflecting on the quality of their work, but they are required to give grades (for example)?

One approach is to define the different grades or marks in terms of different demands being met. Dot Jensen of Jannali Girls High School, NSW, adopts this approach with marks.

> Students receive a mark like 5 for each aspect of the work which we have discussed and get full marks if the task is completed as requested. If an aspect is particularly well done I write a comment saying so. If something is missed I also say so. This eliminates the ranking of students' writing in the range 4 to 8 out of 10, which I have never found very satisfactory.

This is an uncomfortable solution because it is less rigorous than requiring all demands to be met. It lets those students who are content with 4 out of 10 off the hook. It allows them to continue their learning with no record of the specific areas not mastered, and possibly not even understood (as does the traditional grading system).

Because Dot is emphasizing the educational role of assessment, she encourages her students to revise their work, so that they achieve full marks. Of course what then happens is that **many** students get full marks or 'A's. I used this approach with year 9s at Seaton High School and most students got 'A's or 'U's (the bottom grade). This may cause problems with administrators whose understanding of assessment leads them to expect that all subjects should produce the bell-shaped normal curve, regardless of the quality of the students' work and the teaching.

It is a widespread but mistaken view that results should be distributed normally. When they try to require that distribution, administrators often refer to general intelligence being distributed normally: but both the concept, general intelligence, and its supposed normal distribution are **assumptions** made by the mental testing movement, not scientific discoveries. In any case, reference to intelligence is a red herring. It is a simple fact that teaching and learning can be more effective (most students being successful) in some classes and less effective in others (with less being successful). To distort the results of a course to fit a predetermined and arbitrary view of how the results should have been is invalid — and, more seriously, it limits the degree to which teachers can involve students in reflecting on the demands of the subject, which is to say it limits both their incentive and potential to teach. If administrators complain about too many high grades they should be asked to suggest more demanding, educationally sound requirements for the course. If instead they take the results of the learning from the students and distort them, so that those results can no longer be understood by the students, then they are exacerbating the alienation which presently pervades traditional schooling, where students do not often feel a sense of pride in what they have achieved.

DIFFERENT CONTRACTS FOR DIFFERENT GRADES

Another approach to helping students understand a grading system is to have contracts involving different work for the different grades. Extension work can be offered so that students who do extra work are thereby contracting for a higher grade. What I dislike in that system is that plodders get higher grades because of the sheer quantity of work they produce, rather than its quality. Just because Joylene is prepared to spend her weekends doing extra work is no justification to me that she get a higher grade than her sister who spends her weekend socializing.

Sr. Margaret Cain and I tried to spell out alternative tasks which are differentiated, not in terms of the amount of work, but their difficulty. Higher-level tasks were to lead to higher grades. However, we have so far not been able to make justifiable differentiations in terms of difficulty.

For example, we looked at writing about a text at year 11 level. To simply paraphrase the text seemed clearly a low-level task, but we wanted everyone to do more than that. We devised this scheme:

WRITING ABOUT A TEXT

Tasks leading to a 'C'

- Monologue from a character.

- Translation of the content into another genre (e.g. newspaper story, interview with a character).

- Reading journal, but without reader's own questions of the text.

Tasks leading to a 'B'

- Essay answering a set question.

- Dialogue on a topic provided, with two strong voices working towards a resolution.

Tasks leading to an 'A'

- Reading journal with reader's own questions concerning the text and exploration of those questions.

- Dialogues concerning the reader's own questions concerning the text.

- Prediction/sequel.

- Evaluative reactions to the text in terms of clarity, realism, completeness, order, consistency and interest; with detailed reference to the text.

- Why is it important to you? — with precise reference to the text.

- How does this text relate to other reading you've done — with precise reference to the text.

- Imitations or parodies of the writer's style.

The demands of some of these tasks were specified further. We did not offer all the choices at once. We thought we needed to move much more gradually than that.

When we looked at the student's work, the differentiations between the tasks seemed unjustified. One student's monologue from the point of view of one of the characters seemed more perceptive and sophisticated than another's essay and another's evaluative discussion. Consequently, if we considered the monologue a worthwhile task (and we did), we felt we should recognize successful handling of it with more than the limited success of a 'C'.

A second problem with this approach was that the demands of the course were complicated to understand and they were becoming too pervasive a focus, distracting students and teacher from primarily focusing on the text and their responses to them. So I would avoid this approach, because there is too much danger that the course becomes a distasteful drudgery, a sequence of hurdles to be mechanically jumped.

There is also the compromise between grading and work-required assessment, involving the 'M' category for a 'successfully completed product worthy of being used as a model for other students of this year level', which Steve Dowdy discussed in his case study (pp. 134–42).

The distinction between 'M' and 'S' rests on comparison between students' products. 'M' is defined in terms of a concrete use to which the product can be put, namely publication within the school. At Mitcham Girls High School, teachers other than the class teacher act as external judges and stick strictly to that criterion. Consequently, 'M's are quite rare. However, it is possible for there to be many 'M's for a class if their work is very good, especially if the class has worked on a variety of unusual products. Students elect whether to submit their work for external judgement and two external judges must agree for an 'M' to be awarded. When an 'M' is awarded the school publishes the work in some form.

Teachers have suggested another category between 'S' and 'M', but I think that there should be no such further categories. The idea is that 'M' comes to be seen as rather like winning a prize, quite a special event. If there were two gradings above 'S', then 'S' itself would become a relative failure for students with high aspirations. If 'S' comes not to be seen as success, the whole approach reverts to the traditional reality of teachers grading students on largely unstated criteria.

IF NORMAL GRADING IS REQUIRED

When I have been forced to use a normal grading system, grading each piece of work in a much more subjective, unpredictable way without demands being made explicit, I give provisional grades in the first instance and encourage students to rework some of their pieces (usually the better ones). On their work, I sometimes suggest a range of possible grades. For example, 'I think someone who concentrated on the accuracy and relevance of most of your answer and appreciated your attempts to make your language colourful and interesting would give it a 'B'. I think it would get a 'D' from someone who saw your expression as clichéd ('nervous wreck'; 'the murder of Duncan was history now') and focused on your statement that the witches were still around at the end of the play — Where were they?' David Harris provided another example:

> Outstanding clarity; information; depth of ideas; logical development; persuasiveness; use of evidence and style = 19/20 But! ... 15/20 because of changes of tense!

Near the end of a term I get the students to select their best (say) three copies for consideration by an external judge. Because only selected work goes to this final judging and it has been commented upon and possibly reworked, the standard expected for each grade can be higher.

Teachers who are required to produce marks or grades can adapt the approaches discussed here to their own situations, the principles being that:

(1)   much of the work is simply required work: the teacher monitors that students concentrate on and are fully involved in the processes outlined, but other than that no formal judgements of quality are made;

(2)   for selected pieces of work, there will be discussion in class of what constitutes a successful product, and the appropriate demands will be documented for students who might otherwise simply be given a low or middling grade;

(3)   students can rework any product that is judged to be unsuccessful and can 'make up' required work if they are behind — that is, they can **redeem** unsuccesful performances;

(4)   some work is submitted to judges outside the classroom.

STUDENTS' RESPONSES TO THESE APPROACHES

Students who are used to having every piece of work graded find these approaches unusual. In particular, those who have been lucky enough to get very high grades, often for industry, compliance and neatness, sometimes resent the fact that their peers are also able to get quite high grades.

Liz Bowen found this reaction when she applied these approaches in her year 10 English class at Whyalla High School. Twelve weeks after she began, she wrote:

> The students still find it very difficult to accept the scheme of only getting two grades, especially those accustomed to high grades in other subjects and previously in English. this is an issue about which there has been much subsequent discussion with colleagues.

Early in second term I interviewed the students whom Liz described as 'offering the strongest resistance to the extension of deadlines and redeemability of grades'.

Brian: What do you feel about the system of it being up to you to get the work in that will be looked at more closely?

Joan: O.K. We found it easy to get the work in. If you were late, she wouldn't grade it.

Jenny: No, you'd get marks off if you handed it up late.

Sue: I should think so!

Liz reflected: 'They had either consciously or subconsciusly rejected the provisions, speaking as if redeemability did not apply'.

There seems to have been a gradual softening in their attitude. Mid-way through second term, I iz wrote:

> Following class discussion of the claims of a few that the redeemability system was unfair to those who got their work in regularly, the students have generally accepted that these provisions do not in the least affect their own grades and organizational abilities, but rather exist to alleviate the problems of those who do not or cannot organize themselves well, and give them opportunity to improve.

I found year 11s took almost a term before they clearly understood that only their best work need be 'counted'. But when they got the picture they supported the scheme strongly, on grounds of fairness:

Kerin: If you fail on something, you might have been having an off day, but this way you've still got a chance. You don't have to feel flattened.

and on educational grounds:

Briony: I like to experiment and act on different ideas. This system gives you room to experiment. You're not so scared. When you asked us to write about our own questions and confusions in relation to *My Brother Jack* ... in previous years I'd have thought 'That work has to be counted and I might get a U!' ... but knowing it didn't have to count, I was game enough to do it and see how it went. You experiment and you might do really well or not succeed at all. It doesn't matter though. At least you've found out.

USING AN EXTERNAL JUDGE

Referring work to an external judge has become fairly common in South Australian secondary schools, the main advantage being that the

students then more often see the class teacher as an ally, someone to
dicusss and consider work with, not the person who provides the final
answer. As a year 11 student, Lee-anne, said ...

> We talk to you more as a helper ... as an adult to an adult, an equal ... it's
> not like you're talking as a grader, to us as children, all the time. And if we
> get a grudge about our result, it's with the external judge, not you.

Teachers at Playford High School reported that they were indeed
much more helpful to students, when work was going to be judged
externally:[1]

> We are more prepared to give all the help we can. This is very different
> from how we are when our roles as teachers and assessors are confused.
> Then we often find ourselves thinking 'I can see he's got weaknesses in
> this area, but I'll comment on it when I grade it'.
>   Also, when we judge their work we find ourselves *playing the role of an
> outsider* and often this doesn't work with the kids. For example, we might
> say 'Look at this writing! I can't (or won't) read it!' But they know we
> actually do read it when we are helping them, so they don't accept that we
> can't, and feel pushed around if they have to rewrite it. With 'other
> teacher grading' we simply say 'I can read it, but someone else who
> mightn't even notice that it is your work probably isn't going to bother
> wading through it'. It is then up to the student to decide if he will rewrite
> or run the risk.
>
> Sometimes they say 'What do you think it's worth?' I might say 'I think
> maybe a 'C'. I think it needs a better closing paragraph. Do you want to
> change that?' Mostly, the kid rewrites, often three or more drafts. This is
> an unusual experience for me to see it happening so much. Sometimes
> the kid says 'No, I've got too much work to do in the other subjects in the
> next few days'. Then I say 'O.K., let's take a chance and hand it up'.
>   These kids make their own decisions and they are more objective about
> what they deserve. They see the strengths and weaknesses in their work
> after discussing it with me. They aren't playing a game with me of 'What's
> it worth?' where I say 'Rewrite it and I'll give you a better grade'.
>
> I often find myself saying 'I know what you mean because I know you. But
> you need to take your readers by the hand — help them'. I didn't say this
> to kids before. What would have been the point? If I'd understood it and
> no-one else was going to read it, there was no need for revision.
>   Now they are revising, I am able to point out how much improvement
> there is since the first draft — and they see it too.

Students are sometimes anxious because the external judge is likely to
be a more disinterested assessor:

> Briony: At the beginning of the year I didn't like the idea of an external
>   judge at all, because I've always got on well with teachers and
>   got good marks. Now I see it's fairer having someone who
>   doesn't know you.

> If you muck around in class and your teacher doesn't like you, they try to mark it fairly, but it still creeps in; they're more picky with you than someone who behaves well: whereas it's only fair that if you come out with a good essay you should get a good mark. And if you're real good and quiet and the teacher thinks 'She's good, she knows what she's talking about', the teacher gives you better marks but that's not going to help you in the end. With different markers you get more of an idea of what your work is really like.

They usually see writing for the external judge as a more difficult assignment.

> Kerin: Being with a teacher a whole year, you tend to know what to write — what they're looking for. But now we don't think 'It's got to be good for that person', we just try to make *good*. It's harder, but it's a good system.

One of the Playford teachers reported a similar story:

> I'd got used to a lot of the kids' idiosyncrasies of expression. I'd taught most of them before. I just didn't see them anymore. Over a couple of years you get blinder to their faults and increasingly perceptive of their strengths. So it's as much for my benefit as theirs that someone else look at their work.

An external judge saw this as a major advantage of the system ...

> Kids often assume a lot of the reader because they're so used to writing to the teacher, who clearly already knows what they've been discussing in class. When they address themselves to an unknown reader it's more demanding — 'I've got to make the ideas clear and I've got to illustrate them'.

One disadvantage with external judges is that the students often have restricted access to them to discuss their work. Sometimes the judge can come to a lesson. Sr. Margaret Cain and I asked external judges to make tape recordings for the class to listen to, in which they read out strong extracts from the students' work. The class listened very attentively and the students who were quoted probably got a boost from that recognition.

Another danger is that the external judge may embarrass the class teacher by criticizing students' attempts to follow the teacher's advice. I found this very undermining when the conflicting judgement came from a senior person within the school and it disrupted a way of working which was just being established. A teacher from Playford High School described this problem very clearly:

> You teach in your own style to get the kinds of things you think are important across. If another teacher comes along with a different set of values and marks them down for things you've stressed, you lose confidence and the kids lose confidence too.

They start to question your role. Traditionally teachers have been assigned the assessor role. That has been seen as our chief, if not our only, virtue. Once you give away that role you have to work really hard to redefine your own worth within the classroom. It might work very well on a personal, social level, but you've still got that other level, that the kids have got to perceive that you are able to make some sort of judgement of quality. Without that the kids wonder what value your help is. Also they're used to the idea that they'll get a better grade if they follow your advice. If they don't get it they wonder if the help is really relevant.

I don't want the kids to be always thinking 'X likes this style and Y this and I hope to hell I get someone like X in the exam'. Even though it is a bit like this in reality I don't want it thrust upon them all the time. It's a real source of anxiety for them.

Doland Murray[2] wrote 'The writer must listen to the contrary counsel of his readers'. I see that as a valuable part of the learning process, but when it comes time for judgemental assessment, we should try to reduce the likelihood of this sort of contradiction. This can be done by spelling out the demands of tasks so that the students themselves can reflect upon the quality of their work.

Chapters Ten and Eleven have presented ways judgemental assessment can be organized so that students are encouraged rather than discouraged to reflect on the quality of their work themselves. The next chapter outlines some more ways in which teachers foster student reflection, this time by helping the students consider the demands of judgemental assessment.

12 Helping Students to Reflect on the Demands of Judgemental Assessment

If we are committed to assessing in ways which encourage rather than discourage students to reflect on the quality of their own work, then we should be able to explain to them how judgemental assessments are to be arrived at. It is just not good enough to keep judgemental assessment a low key affair, to pretend that it is relatively unimportant, if we are part of a system which tells some students they are unsuccessful. Vaguely progressive teachers who try to gloss over careful attention to the demands of judgemental assessment contribute to a conspiracy which keeps unsuccessful students out in the cold, with no purchase on the assessment process.

The class teacher's role is to help the students prepare for the judgemental situation, that is, to involve them in reflecting on the demands of the curriculum. What this looks like in practice depends on whether the judgements of the students' work are based on work-required assessment or comparisons between students.

REFLECTING ON THE DEMANDS OF A WORK-REQUIRED COURSE

Here is how Jo Hall of Greenwood High School involves students in reflecting on the demands of English B, the course mentioned in Chapter Seven.

Half way through the year I draw up a sheet with a scale numbered 0 to 10 for each requirement, (see examples below). They indicate on these scales how far they think they've got towards completing that piece of work required. 0 means no movement at all and 10 means completion. They do one to keep and one for me. As well, I fill in two for each kid, one copy for me to keep and one for the kid to see.

So I match mine and theirs up and so do they. If there are discrepancies we discuss it straight away. Their sheet and mine are usually pretty much the same. When we don't agree, it's usually because I've forgotten a piece of writing, or they've forgotten to hand something up that they have actually completed.

English B — Mid-Point Assessment
0 = no movement at all 10 = full achievement.
(Examples only)

Writing

Journal — 3 entries per week during writing unit

| 0 | 1 | 2 | 3 | 4 | 5 | 6 | 7 | 8 | 9 | 10 |

Writing analysis

| 0 | 1 | 2 | 3 | 4 | 5 | 6 | 7 | 8 | 9 | 10 |

Good writing statement and self-assessment

| 0 | 1 | 2 | 3 | 4 | 5 | 6 | 7 | 8 | 9 | 10 |

Oral English

Collect, transcribe and analyse data from speech situations

| 0 | 1 | 2 | 3 | 4 | 5 | 6 | 7 | 8 | 9 | 10 |

Identify speaking situtations of particular use to you, practice and prepare a set of guidelines

| 0 | 1 | 2 | 3 | 4 | 5 | 6 | 7 | 8 | 9 | 10 |

After this mid-point assessment their attitude changes. They don't fully grasp till then how the assessment works. Now it becomes clear to them that all there is to it is that they have to complete the goals and be fully involved in the activities. They start to realize for the first time that there's no *hidden*, arbitrary judgements going to come in on the quality of their work. And they now start to be much more responsible for getting there.

It would be good if the change in perception and responsibility came earlier. I've been thinking it would be a good idea to try it half way through first term in future.

Other teachers use check-lists, charts or discussion sessions for this purpose. Maurie Sheehan, an English teacher at Hurstbridge High School, Victoria, discussed this monitoring process:

Before Easter I ask if anyone feels they're not managing and not moving towards accomplishment of the work. This is important and it compares very much with traditional assessment where the students ask the teacher if they're passing. In work-required assessment *they* see the evidence, and that's particularly good for kids who haven't a lot of confidence.

REFLECTING ON THE DEMANDS OF THE CURRICULUM WHEN THE STUDENTS' PRODUCTS ARE TO BE JUDGED AGAINST THOSE OF OTHER STUDENTS

Advice to students who are preparing for judgemental assessment includes 'Don't concentrate so much on experimenting now. Rather, focus on trying to do as good a job as you can, on making a strong impression in the reader's or listener's mind'. The focus is not so much on learning as on a natural end-point of it, when the student is to demonstrate what has been learnt.

Judgements of the worth of students' work are much more emotionally threatening to the students than to us. That much is obvious. What we should not forget is that students will feel much more secure to experiment and take risks, if they are confident that we know the criteria which will apply in the judgement situations and will teach them those criteria.

We often overlook teaching the criteria which are likely to apply to judgements of students' work. Sometimes it is easier to think that the 'good' ones do not need to be told and the 'bad' ones will never understand.

Alistair Dow was reading Dylan Thomas's 'Do not go gentle into that good night' to a year 10 class at Millicent High School. The class asked 'What does it mean?', so Alistair went through the first four lines showning (in his words), 'how you grasp and grope towards your idea, your construction of what it means'. He had intended to stop there, but the class wouldn't let him. He wondered if they were conning him, getting him to do the work for them, but he went on to spend an hour showning them how he read that one poem. At the end the students said 'We've never before seen anyone read a poem. In three years of secondary schooling we've never seen how anyone makes sense of something like that. On our essays we get comments which tell us that we aren't quite on the right track, so we get an A− or a B or a C, but no one has ever shown us what it is that we aren't doing!'

Conscientious teachers often refrain from **showing** students ways to read, write, listen and speak for fear that they will impose a limiting approach on the students. But our approach should not always be to stand back. On the contrary, we should ensure that students see a number of different models of how poetry is read, how good essay answers are written and so on.

Following models is a natural and powerful way of learning and it should not be avoided because of a simplistic belief that all growth in English must be organic, without the benefit of direction or support. We can trust students more than that. If they steadfastly copy a model, that may be providing them with security they need. They will later improvise from the model, thereby making it their own.

Models are probably best introduced after the students have first attempted a genre themselves. Then they can look at them more knowledgeably and more critically.

Some confident students argue quite fairly that their intuitive sense of what is appropriate is more useful to them than specified requirements or models. But it is for the students who are lost, unable to discern what it is they are being asked to do, that we need to give more specific descriptions of what constitutes successful work. On the one hand, we should not be thinking in terms of how their work measures up to **one** ideal answer, but on the other we should be able to give them some fairly clear approaches describing how they could go about succeeding.

Trying to specify these approaches can be a salutary experience for the teacher. To take an actual example, a teacher reflected on a written task she had set her year 11 classes on *Macbeth*. At my suggestion she described the task under five headings: content expected, genre, audience, purpose and level of abstraction. As she described the task she realized that she had not made clear what genre she expected, and that she had not discussed with the students the level of abstraction that was appropriate. She had expected them to show reasoning supported by evidence from the text, but as they were preparing the work, she had encouraged them to express their own opinions of the play. Many of them had done just that, making bold, uncompromising, often naive statements which were genuinely believed and egocentrically expressed with little reference to the play. Clearly, the pieces of writing that resulted could not be taken as evidence that the students were weak in writing about literature, since they had been given no opportunity to internalize the criteria the teacher had been taking for granted.

If students' writing does not show high levels of abstraction, it might be that they have never understood that this is something which is valued in school. Indeed, their teachers might never have clarified this themselves; or the teachers might not have known how to guide the students towards appropriate levels of abstraction. But if more favourable judgements are going to be made of discourse which shows higher levels of abstraction, then we should try to demonstrate how to achieve that.

For example, students might have read *Blubber* by Judy Blume, and the teacher might offer, amongst alternative tasks, the possibility that they write an answer to the question, 'What is the author's message in *Blubber*?'. If the teacher is only concerned to find out their answers, that question is acceptable. But if some students are going to be told that their answers are unsuccessful, then those students deserve clearer guidance as to what strategy they should adopt to produce a successful answer. The teacher has an obligation to help them succeed.

Discussion in class may generate a number of different strategies, one of which might be:

(1) Describe how Linda behaved in the novel.
(2) Highlight the changes in her behaviour and reasons for the changes.
(3) Indicate if you think she is a better person because she changes.
(4) If you know of people like Linda, mention that — would it be good if they changed like Linda did? — Is it realistic to expect that they might?

Notice that this particular strategy goes beyond the question first set. In English we very often reward students for going beyond what the question indicates is wanted. If students would be rewarded for including the fourth step in their answer, then we should tell them that.

AN EXAMPLE: REFLECTING ON THE DEMANDS OF A YEAR 11 ASSIGNMENT

Here is an account of how Sr. Margaret Cain and I tried to help year 11 students understand some of the demands involved in writing about poetry. It illustrates some of the problems which occur when we try to unravel the mystery of what is expected in English.

The students were to write about poetry from a set anthology. This was a requirement we were not free to vary and some of this writing was to be marked by more senior teachers in the school. The students were saying that they found the poetry difficult and that they were confused about what was expected of them. We were concerned that they dwell on the poet's words, taking time to allow meanings to emerge. So we set out some requirements which suggested how they would read the poems.

They were free to choose whatever poem or poems they wished, and in them they were to identify:

- the dominant emotional tone of the poem;
- the dominant image(s);
- associations with that image which help explain its effects;
- the central ideas or message of the poem; and

- separately from those four, they were to indicate their personal evaluation of the poem: 'Your personal feelings will be bound up with what you see under these four headings, but try to separate your evaluation (how it relates to what you know about life) from your understanding of what the poet did with the words.

(This was not the only approach to reading poetry that these students saw during the year.)

First, we talked about some poems in class, simply asking the students to tease out the elements we had outlined. Using this structured approach left plenty of room for discussion, argument and individual decision. At this stage, the structure served more as a focus than a strait-jacket.

We read Robert Frost's *Mending Wall* this way and talked about what they came up with and which parts of the poem triggered their answers. 'What do you get as the emotional tone?' 'Sadness', 'regret', 'mischievousness', 'curiosity', 'arrogance', 'looking down on the neighbour', 'fascination', 'puzzled'; all these seemed to relate to specific parts of the poem. We looked up 'whimsical' in the dictionary, but it did not seem to fit. 'Angry' and 'superstitious' were offerings that seemed to be based on misreadings.

The stone wall was accepted as the dominant image. Associations with the image included 'separation', 'a barrier', 'control', 'owning', 'hiding'.

One student spoke about seeing the wall as made up of people. It seemed to be important to stress 'if you were to write about this one you should make it clear that you know the poet hasn't said that; that is your association'.

Discussing the message of the poem proved a lively affair. We behaved as if there was one best answer to the question, so as to provide a focus for exploring it further.

Later, when it came time to write, we gave the students a sheet which outlined what we were expecting. Under 'content' were repeated the instructions to identify the four elements and to separately describe personal evaluation, as indicated above. Two other headings were:

Structure:
- The writing should have a clear conclusion.

- The writing should have unity: the reader shouldn't be distracted by irrelevant or unnecessary material.

Conventions:
- The reader shouldn't be distracted or confused by idiosyncracies or errors in presentation.

Further, we indicated on the sheet that when it came time for some of their writing about poetry to be judged, 'if your writing satisfies all of these you'll get a B. If it satisfies all of these and is so good that it is worth showing around to other students it gets an A. If it achieves all but one of these it gets a C'.

While they were working on this, we got them in small groups, to indicate what grade would be appropriate for some of their first drafts. The students were able to discuss the work under the terms specified on the sheet and reach a fair degree of concensus as to likely grades, although there was still room for some disagreement.

When they finally presented their work for assessment we felt most of the students produced better work than they had previously. Improvement was least noticeable with those who had already been discussing texts in a confident, accomplished way, but there was certainly no decrease in performance in these students' work.

At the other end of the scale were two essays which finally received passing grades even though they were poorly integrated pieces. The students had mechanically followed our guidelines and these two products were embarrassing for me as someone who recommends spelling out the demands for students in this way. Here is a section of one of these two pieces. The student had chosen to write about George Herbert's 'Virtue'.

'VIRTUE'

I felt the emotion of the poem which the author was trying to get across was one of a depression or pessimistic one, which went to or changed into one of an optermistic or an overwhelming emotion. This was achieved when the author changed from saying no matter how sweet the day, how sweet the rose or how sweet the spring, they all must die. But then went on to say that only a sweet and virtuous soul like a piece of seasoned timber, never dies, only changes and then lives superiarly.

The image I absorbed, from the poem was one of a naked man walking around in a garden observing the sweet bright day, the sweet rose and the spring in the air, and then saying to himself that they will all come to an end sometime. Then he stumbled over a piece of seasoned timber, he picked it up and related his thoughts of the timber closely to that of a soul and saying the soul will never die, only change and live on. I chose a naked man because it represents new born life and to have an opinion of a new born life would be more sensitive and whole-hearted than getting it from someone living in this world.

The message the poet is getting across to the reader is that no matter how sweet anything looks or is, it will gradually come to an end. Whereas our soul forever keeps on changing and chiefly lives just like the piece of seasoned timber.

I enjoyed the poem although it took me quite a while to understand it. It is a short but strong poem with a lot of meanings which relate to our life today. The poet I thought was very clever in the way he symbolized what he wanted to say to the reader and changed the atmosphere of the poem from death to chiefly living.

The thing I thought added the necesary essence to the poem was the information about the piece of timber in relation to the soul.

Ayoub

Following the guidelines specified, the piece was eventually judged worthy of a 'C' grade. Personal evaluation was judged to have been inadequately explained. It was hard to judge 'associations with the dominant image'.

Peter Elbow describes the uneasiness we can feel about work like this: 'We manage to share with students what we know and appreciate ... but their hands are dirty or their fingers are rough. We overhear them saying, "Listen to this neat thing I learned", yet we cringe because they got it all wrong. Best not to share.'[1]

But we **should** share, and we should offer every way into George Herbert that we can. After all George Herbert is not in any danger here! No doubt we could have taught Ayoub a different way — a better way, but when he was struggling at least we offered him some support. I can accept this piece of writing as the best we could manage in working towards a meeting of Ayoub and George Herbert. At the same time, it is also important to think about how we could improve the curriculum to elicit more involvement from him.

I asked the students to comment on the approach of spelling out the demands of a task like this. Most were positive about it, especially those who had not been getting high grades. One such was Christine, who had been absent frequently, had handed up only about half the required work to that point in the year and had received low grades, often because she retold the events of plays and novels rather than discussing them. Christine said:

> I've found this helped me a lot. I haven't known what was expected. If I didn't know we had to do that sort of thing, I would have done nothing ... or I wouldn't have concentrated on the poem so much. I wouldn't have included any of those things if they hadn't been brought up.

Hanna, a student who had been receiving middling grades said:

> Without those requirements, you concentrate on what the poem means to you, not what it says to other people. I think I'll do some of those things when I write about poetry next year, even if the teacher isn't marking the same way. I have this way to fall back on.

But the students who had been receiving high grades were not so keen on this approach. For example, Jo said:

> It became too restricting. It didn't let me show my creativity. I felt I couldn't go too much into discussing *all* the images and what they meant.

Even so, I did get something out of this idea of making it clear which associations with the image are sort of part of the poem, not just your own associations to it.

Some students suggested that they could be allowed to choose, either to be judged on criteria which had been explained, or if they felt that limited them to be judged without specific reference to those criteria.

Christine: It's a good idea. It should be optional. People who don't know what to write about will use it. There'll only be a few who feel limited by it, but they can explore things in their own way if they want to and choose to take the risk and be judged without quite knowing on what basis.

This seems like sound advice. Further than that, students who have been shown different ideas of what can be required in a particular genre, could elect to choose the approach they felt suited them most, or even to describe what they were trying to do in terms selected from different approaches.

Finally students' involvement in reflecting on the demands of the tasks can be made quite explicit by getting those who seem to be having trouble to check off on a cover-note, each of the demands which they consider they have successfully addressed. This reminds them to read their work with those demands in mind and can alert the classroom teacher to situations where the demands are misunderstood.

Appendix 3 presents five more examples of teachers defining the demands of tasks in English, to act as guides to reflection on what constitutes successful and unsuccessful performance.

The emphasis of this book on spelling out demands that are to apply to particular, selected products is based on a rejection of general impression marking and use of analytic scales,[2] because both these approaches leave the students in the dark about what they need to do to succeed.

Articulating the demands of tasks in English is what is done in primary trait scoring.[3] Odell[4] recently discussed two drawbacks of this approach.

Firstly, students who take unusual but worthwhile approaches to a particular task might be unfairly penalized. This problem applies in the examination room, but it is not a great difficulty when the approaches described in the book are used. Teachers can decide to refer to defined demands only when students' work is considered unsuccessful — or they can apply the demands to every student's work, in which case, students who come up with unusual products may need also to satisfy the demands, in another piece. Because only selected, polished pieces are to be looked at in terms of demands, unusual approaches involve no irredeemable penalty for the writer.

Odell sees as another drawback with primary trait scoring, that aspects like cohesion and mechanics can be overlooked. But teachers need not overlook these things when they define the demands which are appropriate to polished pieces. For example, final copy can be required to be free of error — as is the case in English B. Further, while it is **usually** inappropriate to tell students that first draft material should be free of spelling errors, for example (because this would restrict their word choice), there are some situations in which correct spelling is important in first draft writing, and as long as students know precisely when this will be required, it can be a demand.

13 Implications for Records, Reports, Student Promotion and State-Wide Examining Practices

---

Discussions of assessment often focus on reports the school makes to parents and employers, and on state-wide examining procedures. In contrast, this book has focused on assessment and its effects within the classroom. Even so the approach to assessment described here has some clear implications for the related matters of records, reports, promotion and state-wide examining.

RECORDS

Record keeping within the class has been discussed in Chapters Six, Nine and Twelve. What of records over a longer period which could be used to monitor long-term growth? Chapters Two and Five argued the principle that reflections on students' work be based on the particulars of the work itself, not on teachers' conceptualizations of it. Following that argument, the most useful record to keep is a folio or file of a small number of selected, polished pieces, be they written or spoken on cassette. Four or five products a year is plenty. These folios can serve as a very positive record of achievement, they can be a reference point for showing growth over five or six years and can be something which the students develop pride in. As a teacher from Playford High School said:

Keeping a few polished pieces means that we also protect ourselves in the face of critics who focus only on the product rather than the writing process! We have good products to show them!

That these records emphasize the students' best work is appropriate for the same reasons as applied to judging the work: the students are given an achievable goal and are free to experiment in classroom work without having to feel that they may be held accountable for failed experiments at a later date. Few would suggest that photography folios, for example, should contain rejected work, over-exposures and so on: yet because schools are so used to examining writing for evidence of failure to learn, some claim that the emphasis on the best writing is invalid or unfair.

Folios of selected pieces of writing are used at Noble Park Technical College, Victoria, where they contain:

> samples of work prepared by each student. A trade teacher concerned about the kids' chances of employment suggested these folios. They do look good, and provide concrete examples of the students' competences'.[1]

Work in the folios can be the focus of discussion with parents. This provides a clear ground for the discussion and the parents are often very reassured when they find that the teacher cares enough to know their child's work and talk articulately about it. Students can also use the folio or file, particularly near the end of their schooling for showing to an employer, and they should be able to select from it as they choose.

While the students are attending school, the teachers will have some measure of ownership of the folios, so that they can consider them, alongside the documented course requirements, in reviewing the quality and balance in the English teaching throughout the school. Rarely does a school systematically reflect on the five years or so of English teaching which it offers: inarticulate record systems based on marks and grades provide no information which can be used for this purpose. Of course the sample of work provided by the folios is a highly selected one, but it is a practical option because students and teachers will care about collecting the work; and it will always be accessible to teachers who are concerned to detect biases and omissions in the teaching provided over the span of a student's time at the school.

As an example of what a review of the curriculum can show, Graham Little[2] has described how a bias often develops such that students' talking and writing concentrate on the material world and neglect the figurative and the abstract. As a result, students know words like diameter and parallel but not dilemma and paradox. Similarly, biases can occur in the audiences for students' speaking and writing, or there may be a lack of balance between informal and formal language tasks.

So students will need to know that teachers may use the folios in this way. When they leave school the students should be free to take the folios with them.

A further record is provided by the comments assembled according to any of the systems described in Chapter Six. it would be easy to place the record sheets or the pages from the student's work-book in the folio at the end of each year. Inevitably, by the end of the year, some students will have lost their folders and there is little we can do about that.

Records of students' engagement in the curriculum (Chapter Three), involvement in writing and reading processes (Chapters Four and Eight), and the readers' responses (Chapter Five) should not be kept. It is simply not worth the time and effort that it would require because those things very much depend on the context of the particular class and are an ongoing responsibility of each teacher.

REPORTING

Chapter Ten provides an example of a report form (p. 133) which is easy for the teacher to complete and yet provides more information about what students are doing than is common in school reports.

Many teachers prefer to comment further on individual students' work. The forms provide room for that. As was argued in Chapter Two, these comments should focus on students' strengths and goals, not on their attitude or behaviour, and the assembled comments (Chapter Six) make this a straightforward task.

If the English teachers are required to write only a few lines on a school-wide report sheet, then 'successfully completed the require-ments' or 'did not complete the requirements', perhaps with a very brief description of the course, is appropriate. Hopefully the school will allow the more detailed English report to go home stapled to the school sheet, but if not it will have to go separately, and a copy be filed in the students' folios.

Reports to employers can use the same form, but should relate to work in the last year only. The students may support that with work from their folio.

In South Australia, some employers demand that students bring school report forms to job interviews so that they can examine grades for attitude and achievement over the whole of the students' secondary schooling. Students should be protected from that. Reports which describe what students actually do at school, rather than how they are judged, will reduce the likelihood of that abuse.

STUDENT PROMOTION

The approaches to judging, recording and reporting that are presented here make teachers much more accountable for what they do. This is one factor that administrators like. Students are also more accountable.

Their contract is more clearly specified and they bear much of the responsibility for achieving it.

As was discussed in Chapter Ten, we would expect most students to successfully complete their courses once the requirements are defined for them, especially given that they can call on the teacher's help. However, some students clearly choose not to engage in school courses. While we must continually endeavour to adapt our courses to best help the students, we must also accept that some students deliberately avoid satisfying requirements, sometimes so as to pay back parents who have insisted that they stay on at school. When this happens in secondary school, it is only appropriate that they experience the consequences of their actions. So some students will not successfully complete courses and where certain courses are prerequisites for later courses they will not be able to attempt the later ones. Specifiying the requirements of courses will help us decide when prerequisites are in fact justifiable.

When I taught year 9 for a year at Seaton High School, one boy worked quite effectively, but deliberately avoided completing defined requirements. He repeated year 9 English the next year — and the year after that! Both he and his peers clearly understood that he chose to do this, that it was not a matter of him being stupid, or even that his work was of poor quality.

That this occasionally happens is regrettable, but I think students have a right to be confronted with the consequences of their actions. No punishment is required.

To routinely promote students to subsequent courses regardless of their involvement in justifiable prerequisites is a crazy system. Assertions that everyone should always pass are based on woolly thinking which insufficiently acknowledges the students' responsibility to take part in their education. I recently saw a draft of a policy statement which argued that 'where the child begins and ends in relation to other children or to arbitrarily determined standards is irrelevant'. That much is true: but the processes and product demands which English teachers make should not be arbitrary. They should be based on their knowlege of the subject and their students. When they are justifiable and responsible demands, they can be insisted upon as necessary for successful completion of the course.

STATE-WIDE EXAMINING PRACTICES

In South Australia, students in the final year of school (year 12) who want to win university entrance take subjects which are administered by a state-wide examining authority. Their results in these subjects, (referred to as publicly examined subjects) are determined by a combination of marks from a state-wide examination and marks from course work during the year.

Locally there has been much discussion about what relative weightings should be given to each component, the exam and the course work. In the past, course work has contributed 25%, and the examination 75%, but this is soon to change to a 50:50 mix. However, this debate has been rather pointless: the internal school assessments are moderated against the examination results which consequently are the major determinant of the final result.

More emphasis on the class teacher's assessments has been seen as a progressive step, yet, as was argued in Chapter Two, this often means that students are liable to be judged throughout the year. The approach recommended in this book suggests that course work marks should focus on selected pieces of work which are reworked to a high level of quality, with teacher help, and then submitted to a small panel of assessors.

Perhaps the class teacher might be a member of this panel, to act as an advocate for each student and to explain the criteria for assessment which have been discussed in class. However, the situation should be avoided where the class teacher is the one who advantages some and disadvantages others, because the class teacher is inevitably influenced by knowledge of how the student has worked throughout the year. The students should know that what happens within the class is to be treated more confidentially than that. Without this confidentiality, ambitious students perform for the judge throughout the year, giving particular attention to producing work which pleases the teacher and includes that teacher's suggestions. Imagine you are in such a class, and the teacher who will determine your course mark suggests a major change to your work which you don't agree with. If you are very keen to do well, what would you do? Many students try to give the teacher what he or she wants without necessarily being convinced that the work will thereby be improved. In doing so they sell out. They are focusing on what they think is wanted, and not on their own judgement of the work.

In both South Australia and Victoria, the state examining authority also accredits and oversees the assessment of courses which use the assessment structures recommended in this book.

Some of these courses produce grades which are arrived at totally within the school following the guidelines recommended here, namely:

(1) much of the work is simply required work: the teacher monitors that students concentrate on and are fully involved in the processes outlined, but other than that no formal judgements of quality are made;

(2) for selected pieces of work, there will be discussion in class of what constitutes a successful product, and the appropriate demands will be documented for students who might otherwise have simply been given a low or middling grade:

(3) students can rework any product that was judged to be unsuccessful and can 'make up' required work if they are behind. That is they can **redeem** unsuccessful performances;

(4) some work is submitted to judges outside the classroom.

Other accredited year 12 subjects use work-required assessment as described in Chapter Ten. Students are assessed to have 'successfully completed' or 'not completed' them. In South Australia they are called Community Studies subjects and students can negotiate much of what they will work on within the prescribed learning processes which define the course. The Community Studies subjects are mostly inter-disciplinary and often involve work outside the school.

These work-required assessed courses are gaining a positive reputation for providing an environment in which students develop confidence and present work which is superior to what they have previously produced.

At the same time these courses are very much 'second choice' subjects because they do not qualify students for university entrance. So students going into year 12 choose between these and the competitive assessment structure. It is, in the main, the students who feel that they would do poorly in exam-orientated subjects, who take these alternative courses; many of them would not have stayed on at school till year 12 a few years ago.

Some of these students still manage to win entry into university by presenting themselves, with folders of their work, to universities who have alternative entry provisions which are open to school leavers; but it would be very difficult for them to get direct entry into courses like medicine and law for which the competition is most intense.

I hope that as the educational reputation of these courses grows, we see the prerequisites for university entrance change. For example, students could be required to take one or two subjects which are structured in a work-required, co-operative assessment mode alongside their more traditional exam-orientated subjects.

In the meantime, it is often argued that because many students are destined to undergo the exam-orientated, competitive assessment structure in year 12, so they should experience this assessment structure earlier in their secondary schooling. This is a very superficial line of argument indeed.

In work-required assesed courses, students learn to clarify and then satisfy the demands of the course requirements. It is just this ability to take responsibility for their own learning which is lacking in many students presenting for final year subjects at school: at least that is the complaint I hear most commonly from teachers at this level.

Most teachers I know who use work-required assessment, think that it provides a much more effective context for learning than does the traditional assessment structure. If this proves to be generally true in the years ahead, then students of these courses will be at an advantage by the time they begin their final year at school. Such students understand that when they take on an exam-orientated subject, they are submitting themselves to a different assessment structure. They are capable of finding out what the demands of such subjects are and of organizing themselves accordingly.

They also talk to their teachers, as they go through secondary school, about their suitability for the academic demands of exam-orientated courses. And, their teachers offer the best advice they can, but without recording this as gradings or categorizations on school reports, which are to serve other purposes.

The establishment of work-required assessed courses as a solid alternative to traditional, judgementally assessed senior school courses is often threatened by administrators who support the new courses, but fail to understand the centrality of the assessment approach. These people often argue that a common set of grades or scores should apply to both exam-orientated and work-required courses so that both types of subject will be seen to be of equal status by audiences of the year 12 certificate. However parity of esteem cannot be quaranteed by a cosmetic change to the assessment categories. When this is attempted, the unique educational climate of the work-required assessment courses is largely destroyed and the teachers who worked hard to develop roles beyond the limited ones required in the traditional assessment structures see much of their work wasted, because of a misguided egalitarianism.

Appendix 1: Subsidiary Findings of the Initial Research Study (reported on pp. 4–8)

The student questionnaire provided us with the opportunity to investigate three other questions concerning student response to assessment schemes. We asked the students to indicate the reasons they thought the teacher had for assessing them, by choosing from a list provided in the questionnaire. We thought students involved in a responsive approach might more often indicate that it was to help them improve, whereas the students under the judgemental sytem might more often see its purpose to be to check on the amount they work, to allow the teacher to see how each student compares with the rest of the class or merely to satisfy a requirement of teaching as a job.

However, there was no relationship between responsiveness and the reasons chosen by the students. Most attributed a helping, educational intention to their teachers, and this was true under each assessment approach.

We also examined the degree to which the students saw their assessment schemes to be fair. Four items from the questionnaire formed a reliable scale to indicate this aspect of the students' response. We suspected that students under the judgemental scheme might be more satisfied that they were treated fairly than the students under the responsive schemes, for the concept of fairness, which is of the essence in a judgemental approach, is given less importance in a responsive approach. For example, in a judgemental scheme, the teacher does not allow a student to revise a piece of work after it has been graded and then have it regraded, because this would be 'unfair'. In contrast, the responsive teacher would see the educational value of the revision to be the most important consideration.

However, our suspicion was contradicted. The Pearson correlation coefficient between responsiveness and fairness was .33 ($df = 32, p <$ .05), indicating a statistically significant, although small, relationship such that the responsive schemes were described as fairer than were the judgemental schemes.

Another interesting question was whether the students in the judgemental approach were more inclined to interpret their assessments in a competitive way. (Have I beaten my friends, or have they beaten me?) This was assessed in questions like these: 'When your work is returned are you more interested in finding out how your work compares with others in the class, or would you rather know what the teacher thought was good and what could be improved?', 'You receive a better assessment than previously — does this mean that your work is better than that which you usually produce, or that you are closer to the top of the class?'

There was indeed a negative correlation between responsiveness and a competitive orientation amongst the students (the Pearson coefficient was $-.51, df = 32, p < .01$). Students working under a judgemental scheme reported a competitive approach more frequently, whereas those in the more responsive approaches were more concerned with comparing assessment information with what they had received previously.

Further analysis confirmed that this latter finding concerning competitiveness could not be explained in terms of teacher popularity or student achievement (assessed, as before, in terms of teacher grades).

Appendix 2: 'Showing How You Read': A Detailed Example

The longest tape I've made was of my reading of this piece by a year 9 boy.

IT WASN'T THE FIRST TIME ... AND IT WON'T BE THE LAST — BUT IT NEARLY WAS!

The dog lay on the old wooden verandah, completely motionless. Quietly a chair is moving, back and forth, back and forth. In the chair is an elderly man, dozing in the shade of the verandah. He is simply dressed in a shirt that has been out of fashion since the early fifties, so too are his trousers. His hands are old and leathery, his face is wrinkled. Like the surrounding dunes. The only noise that reaches one's ears, is that of the flies — or is it? A door on the derelict shed is moving on it's hinge, as a wind blows through the area — in fact, it's the only door. A lizard darts from the old groaning water-bore, seeking shelter on the barren land.

My response to Chris:

Chris, well, even after the first lines I can say what I'm thinking. It's very much like a movie where I look at the dog and that's all I can see and then I can hear the chair moving back and forth and then I'm turning and looking at that, and there in the chair is an elderly man dozing in the shade of the verandah and it's as if in this opening paragraph I'm looking at each thing very slowly and carefully and that reinforces this idea of it being, oh how can I say it? It's still. I know there's movement but it's sort of still and quiet and you're making us linger over each of these things.

And you say 'the only noise that reaches one is that of the flies — or is it?' Or is it the flies, I guess that is. It's a bit ambiguous as to what that means. I guess that's what you're after there.

I'm not quite sure if that's a hundred per cent right or if it sounds a bit like an idea tacked on to try and reinforce the impression of it being derelict, more than you need.

The birds won't land here! You see everything is black — black, black. Grey smoke rises from the ground, black — sheep carcases scatter the paddocks, only a few move in aggonizing pain.

Down the dirt road, to the right are a pair of fire engines, disappearing in a cloud of dust, to fight the man made flame.

I wonder about grey smoke, whether that should be black if everything's black, but I'm not sure. It's nit-picking probably.

The exhausted fire-crews can't stop at all the burning properties, they're in a race with the fuel-eating giant.

A **pair** *of fire engines [laughing]. That's funny, a pair ... disappearing in a cloud of dust, to fight the man made flame! Yeah.*

O.K. Well the next short paragraph is a new scene in this sort of picture you're showing us.

The farmers, stand in their yards. Their eyes full of desperation — their very existance turning to ash.

'Turning to ash'! That's pretty good. Pretty strong.

Confused, panic striken people walk blindly, through the intensly thick smoke. Many of them have no possessions.

Those who have put their personal losses aside, are working for the towns survival. Petrol is being put into a pit, the drums won't explode if they're underground. Gutters are being filled-up with water. Women and children are being moved to the old, white-wash hotel, in the middle of the town.

'Many of them have no possessions' leaves it a bit up in the air. Do you mean they're not carrying their possessions? Or many of them no longer have any possessions. 'Confused, panic stricken people walk blindly' ... **walk** *blindly. Walk seems a bit weak there. Whether they'd run or dash or stumble or walk or grope, I don't know.*

This is great. This shows a detailed understanding of this situation in you, which makes it seem so real, because of the detail.

There are two fire trucks on the out-skirts of the town, one's at the south-eastern corner, the other's at the south-western.

You're writing this very simply and descriptively. You could almost say starkly. It's a bit like Henry Lawson.

They're preparing for the final duel with this destructor of life. ———— *That's pretty strong again — 'final duel'. 'There are two fire trucks.' Now we had two fire trucks before I think ... 'A pair of fire engines' and so it's a little lacking in tightness, before we had two fire **engines** ... and now there are two fire **trucks** and you bothered to tell us precisely where they are, preparing for the final duel and so it leaves a doubt in my mind as to whether these are the same trucks as what you were calling engines before.*

The hoses are layed out on the ground, the water tanks full. All they can do is wait. Yes, wait for it to come. *It might be good to have left that vague, because it's making it then very general. On the other hand when I first read it, I was thinking, well the hoses aren't waiting. I'm not sure. I have those two reactions there. By not specifying who they are, it could make it stronger or, on the other hand, I can also see it as not utterly clear who they are, and it can seem a bit as if it's the hoses laid out on the ground and the water tanks that are full are the ones that wait.*

A siren's getting closer, lights are just visible through the smoke — the third engine has arrived. ———— *The third engine has arrived **could** be really strong, but, there's been no reference to another engine, we're not waiting for one or thinking that it's not going to come, or that it's been burnt or something like that, which would make it strong if we were thinking 'Isn't it a pity it can't come? Ah! It's come! The third engine!' So **the** third engine; **a** third engine has arrived — is as much as I get out of it.*

The day is turning to night: the sky is turning to a fiery orange, the hot wind is blowing the smoke away — but the danger still remains.

... Yes, the elderly man has seen it all before.

by Chris Northeast

Well, that's quite a stunning little ending. 'Yes, the elderly man has seen it all before' and I go back to the beginning: 'It wasn't the first time ... and it won't be the last — but it nearly was'. Right. It makes it all tie together for me, which is pretty good. 'The danger still remains' leaves a bit of a question in my mind, which I guess is what you're trying to do there. Does the danger still remain from this particular day and fire, or that more fires will come? As you say it won't be the last, in the title.

Anyway Chris, ... I thought I'd have more to say, but that's about it.

This tape took nine minutes to make (reading aloud and comments).

Appendix 3: Defining the Demands of Tasks in English: More Examples

1. Anne Hoogendoorn offered her year 9 students at Wanniassa High School the option of choosing a task for which the damands were clearly defined. All those who chose it satisfied the requirements and wrote more effectively than Anne had expected. This was the task:

   Read again the first chapter of *All the Green Year* by D. E. Charlwood. The author begins 'The year I remember best from those days is 1929'. He does various things in this chapter:

   (i) he gives all the significant reasons why he remembers this year so well.
   (ii) he introduces his main characters *and their relationship to him* (Johnno, Moloney, Father, etc.).
   (iii) he hints at some interesting developments in the plot ('fiasco at its end', 'final disgrace').
   (iv) he includes anecdotes (the problem of Grandfather McDonald and their decision to move).
   (v) he begins to establish the setting.

   Your task
   Imagine you are writing a novel — 'an imagined autobiography' about **one** year of your life. You are to select one year, e.g. 1978, 1981, and write the first chapter of this book in a similar style to D.E. Charlwood. You should do all of the things he did (points i–v). Remember you

write best from your own experience particularly using a familiar setting, even if you change events and people's names, etc. Use your life experiences *and* your imagination! I hope you enjoy doing it. It should be at least 800 words. (One page of D.E. Charlwood's is approximately 280.)

2. Work reported by the London Association for the Teaching of English in their discussion pamphlet, *Assessing Compositions*[1] leads to a set of demands for **imaginative writing**.

   (i)   The experience described seems real. Relevant detail shows that the writer is creating or recreating an experience, not bordering on cliché.

   (ii) The work is structured so that the experience described has significance for the writer and reader. there may be a simple change of pace. There may be a sense of coming to the point in the narrative for which all before has prepared, and on which all that follows reflects.

   (iii) Spelling and punctuation are adequately controlled so that the writer manages to communicate without confusing or irritating the reader excessively.

3. Cooper's work[2] on **personal narrative** suggests a set of demands like these:

   (i)   *Author's role*: The writer keeps to a role, either as participant or observer throughout.

   (ii) *Style or voice*: The writer gives the impression of stating what he/she thinks and feels.

   (iii) *Central figure*: The main person is described in sufficient detail so that he/she seems real.

   (iv) *Background*: The action ocurs in a place you can almost see because of the detail the writer has given.

   (v)   *Sequence*: The order of events is clear, even if the writer talks about the past or the future.

   (vi) *Theme*: The writer gives a sense of why the subject is important to him or her, either by direct explanation or more subtly.

4. Work done by Bracewell, Bereiter and Scardamadia[3] suggests the following as a possible set of demands for students' **writing on topical issues**. The student indicates:

   (i)   what he or she believes;
   (ii) why he/she believes that;
   (iii) what people who disagree believe;
   (iv) why they are wrong or reasons for their beliefs; and
   (v)   his or her conclusions.

As Mike Dilena has pointed out,[4] 'A variety of more complex and interesting "frames" or models can be deduced from articles that deal with controversial issues. Having recognized that readers hunger for order and that good writers provide clear signposts that point the way to their conclusions, students can begin to exploit their reading to learn strategies for writing'.

5. Cooper's work[5] on dramatic writing might lead to the following demands being defined:

   (i)   That both conversation and stage directions be used.
   (ii) Structure: The opening lines invite further reading.
             Incidents are sequenced in a comprehensible (non-arbitrary) way.
             The resolution is believable.
   (iii) Characters are credible. They show consistency and some development as well.
   (iv) It is clear who is speaking at any time.

Notes and References

1 ASSESSMENT AND STUDENT REFLECTION

1. Di Bills, Rob Brown, Michael Cowling, Rod Dinning, Jane Hiatt, Geraldine McOmish, Bruno Phalke and Lawrie Stevens.
2. B. Johnston, 'Responding to students writing' in M.J. Lawson and R. Linke (ed.), *Inquiry and Action in Education*. Adelaide: AARE, 1981.
3. B. Johnston, 'Motivational effects of different assessment schemes in secondary English' in R.D. Eagleson (ed.), *English in the Eighties*. Adelaide: AATE, 1981.
4. B. Johnston, 'Motivational effects of different schemes for assessing students' writing', *Pivot*, 1980, 7, 3, 61–64 and 1981, 8, 1, 10–13.
5. D. A. Kolb, I. M. Rubin and J.M. McIntyre, *Organisational psychology: an experiential approach*. Englewood Cliffs, New Jersey: Prentice Hall, 1979.
6. Both statements are taken from D. Tomlinson, B. Godwin, A. Dragicevich and M. Swain, 'Assessment and the implications of failure'. Paper presented at the Third International Conference on the Teaching of English, 18–22 August, 1980, University of Sydney.
7. P. Broadfoot, *Assessement, schools and society*. London: Methuen, 1979, p. 113.
8. B. Johnston, 'Understanding others and effectiveness in educational groups'. Unpublished PhD thesis, University of Adelaide, 1978, Chapter 12.
9. M.C. Kirkland, 'The effects of tests on students and schools'. *Review of Education Research*, 41, 1971.
10. M.V. Covington and R.G. Beery, *Self-worth and school learning*. New York: Holt, Rinehart and Winston, 1976. The earlier material on failure-avoidance is also based on Covington and Beery's work.
11. M.R. Lepper and D. Greene, *The hidden costs of reward*. Hillsdale, New Jersey: Lawrence Erlbaum, 1978.

12. The relevance of this passage to school work and assessment was pointed out by M. Montgomery, 'Grading and assessment'. *Issues in Higher Education*, no. 1, Autumn, 1977, Westhill College, Birmingham.
13. Hextall, 'Marking work' in G. Whitty and M. Young (eds), *Explorations in the politics of school knowledge*. Nafferton: Naggerton Books, 1976.
14. A.F. Osborn, *Applied Imagination*. New York: Scribners, 1957.
15. Sawkin, cited in J.R. Squire, 'Composing — a new emphasis for the schools' in W.T. Petty and P.J. Finn (eds), *The writing process of students*. Buffalo, New York: State University of New York at Buffalo, 1975.
16. V. Woolf, *A Writer's Diary*. London: Hogarth Press, 1953.

2 DO SCHOOLS' ASSESSMENT STRUCTURES ENCOURAGE STUDENTS TO REFLECT ON THEIR LEARNING?

1. H. Black and P. Broadfoot. *Keeping track of teaching: Assessment in the modern classroom*. London: Routledge and Kegan Paul, 1982, p. 70.
2. Patricia Broadfoot, 'The Scottish Pupil Profile System' in T. Burgess and E. Adams, *Outcomes of education*. London: Macmillan Education, 1980. Vince Catherwood, 'Assessment: The New Zealand Experience'. Paper presented to the Third International Conference on the Teaching of English, Sydney, August, 1980.
3. Black and Broadfoot, *Keeping track of teaching: Assessment in the modern classroom*.
4. Ibid.
5. Donald Greaves, quoted in P. Ryan, 'Donald Greaves on Children's Writing', *News and Views*, 1980, 2, 48–51.
6. Catherwood, 'Assessment: The New Zealand Experience', p. 13.

3 MONITORING THE STUDENTS' RELATIONSHIP TO THE SUBJECT MATTER

1. Betty Jean Wagner. *Dorothy Heathcote: Drama as a learning medium*. London: Hutchinson, 1979.
2. Ibid., p. 71.
3. Ibid., p. 76.
4. Ibid., p. 58.
5. Jon Cook, 'Negotiating the curriculum: programming for learning' in Garth Boomer (ed.), *Negotiating the curriculum: a teacher–student partnership*. Sydney: Ashton Scholastic, 1982.
6. Jo-Anne Reid. 'Negotiating education' in Garth Boomer (ed.), *Negotiating the curriculum: a teacher-student partnership*.
7. Thomas Gordon's *Teacher Effectiveness Training* (New York: Peter Wyden, 1974) is helpful here.

8. I have discussed this understanding of self-assessment further in 'Encouraging productive self assessment', *English in Australia*, 1982, 59, 31–39 and 'Self-assessment in practice: a problem solving approach to writing', *Developments in English Teaching*, 1983, 2, 1, 14–41.
9. Peter Medway. *Finding a language: Autonomy and learning in school.* Richmond, Surrey: Writers and Readers Publishing Co-operative, 1980, p. 6.

4 HELPING STUDENTS TO REFLECT ON THEIR WRITING PROCESSES

1. James Moffett, *Active Voice: a writing program across the curriculum.* Montclair, New Jersey: Boynton/Cook, 1981, p. 29–48.
2. Ibid., p. 30.
3. Peter Elbow, *Writing without teachers.* New York: Oxford University Press, 1973.
4. Peter Elbow, *Writing with power: Techniques for mastering the writing process.* New York: Oxford University Press, 1981.
5. Ken Macrorie, *Searching writing: a context book.* Rochelle Park, New Jersey: Hayden, 1980, p. 6.
6. A.F. Osborn, *Applied imagination.* New York: Scribners, 1957.
7. James Moffett, *Coming on centre: English education in evolution.* Montclair, New Jersey: Boynton/Cook, 1981.
8. James Moffett, *Active Voice*, p. 32.
9. Donald Graves, *Writing: teachers and children at work.* Exeter, New Hampshire: Heinemann, 1983, p. 6.
10. James Moffett, *Coming on centre*, p. 140.
11. Pat Craddock of Syndal Technical School, Victoria.
12. Lola Brown, 'It's not just an ordinary old life: writers as readers', *English in Australia*, 1983, 64, 21–25.

5 HELPING STUDENTS BECOME BETTER READERS OF THEIR OWN WRITING

1. Donald Murray, *Learning by teaching: selected articles on writing and teaching.* Montclair, New Jersey: Boynton/Cook, 1982, pp. 164–72.
2. Peter Elbow, *Writing without teachers.* New York: Oxford University Press, 1973.
3. Bernard Newsome. 'The nature and importance of narrative', *Idiom*, Summer, 1979, 20–23.
4. W. Labov, *Language in the inner city.* Philadelphia: University of Pennsylvania Press, 1973.

6 HELPING STUDENTS IDENTIFY STRENGTHS IN THEIR WRITING AND GOALS FOR IMPROVEMENT

1. This is an extract from 'So many good intentions: organizing what will happen to students' writing in English classes', *Curriculum Exchange*, Trinity Term, 1983, pp. 27–41.

7 HELPING STUDENTS TO ASSESS THEIR OWN WRITTEN PRODUCTS

1. *English B (Group 2): Higher School Certificate Course Description*. Melbourne: Victorian Institute of Secondary Education, 1983, p. 20.
2. Ibid., p. 19.
3. Ibid., p. 20.

8 HELPING STUDENTS TO REFLECT ON THEIR READING

1. Bryant Fillion, 'Reading as inquiry: an approach to literature learning', *English Journal*, January 1981, pp. 39–45.
2. Quoted in Anthony Adams and Ted Hopkin, *Sixth Sense: English — a case study*. Glasgow: Blackie, 1981, pp. 129–30.
3. Patricia Murphy, 'The value of drama as a response to poetry', *Opinion*, 1983, 12, 2, 24–28.
4. Jim Dellitt, '"Hamlet" at year 11: Allowing students space to "pluck out the heart of the mystery"', *Opinion*, 1982, 11, 2, pp. 23–27.
5. Heather Carey. 'Respond to "Hamlet" by writing Hamlet's journal', *Opinion*, 1982, 11, 2, 28–34.
6. Peter Adams, 'Responding to reading — what kinds of writing?' in *A single impulse: Developing responses to literature*. Adelaide: Education Department of South Australia, 1984.
7. Suggested in B. Fillion, 'Reading as inquiry', p. 43.
8. Peter Adams, *Revealing more than we can tell* and *Speaking more truly than they know*. Elizabeth, South Australia: Education Department of South Australia, Central Northern Region, 1982.
9. From Peter Adams, *Revealing more than we can tell*.
10. David Mallick. 'Children's writing: embryonic literature in the classroom, in R.D. Walshe, Dot Jensen and Tony Moore (eds), *Teaching Literature*. Rozelle, N.S.W.: PETA/ETA (N.S.W.), 1983.

10 ORGANIZING JUDGEMENTAL ASSESSMENT I

1. P. Elbow, 'Embracing contraries in the teaching process', *College English*, 1983, 45, 4, 327–39.

2. B. Johnston, 'Work required assessment', *The Australian Teacher*, 1985, 14, 11–19.
3. Bill Hannan and David McRae were key figures in its implementation.
4. P. Elbow, 'Embracing contraries', p. 335.

11 ORGANIZING JUDGEMENTAL ASSESSMENT II

1. Excerpts from J. Cooke, M. Cowling, B. Johnston and J. Manuel, 'An evaluation of other teacher grading', *English in Australia*, 1982, 59, 60–9.
2. Donald Murray, *Learning by teaching. Selected articles on writing and teaching.* Montclair, New Jersey: Boynton Cook, 1982.

12 HELPING STUDENTS TO REFLECT ON THE DEMANDS OF JUDGEMENTAL ASSESSMENT

1. P. Elbow, 'Embracing contraries in the teaching process', *College English*, 1983, 45, 4, 330.
2. P. Diederich, *Measuring growth in English*. Urbana, Illinois: NCTE, 1974.
3. R. Lloyd-Jones, 'Primary trait scoring of writing' in C.R. Cooper and L. Odell, (eds), *Evaluating writing: describing, measuring, judging*. Urbana, Illinois: NCTE, 1977; C. Greenlagh and D. Townsend, 'Focussed holistic scoring', *Language arts*, 1981, 58, 7, 811–22.
4. L. Odell, 'Defining and assessing competence in writing' in C.R. Cooper, (ed.), *The nature and measurement of competency in English*. Urbana, Illinois: NCTE, 1981.

13 IMPLICATIONS FOR RECORDS, REPORTS, STUDENT PROMOTION AND STATE-WIDE EXAMINING PRACTICES

1. Education Department of Victoria, *Changing assessment and reporting procedures: Learning in Humanities*. Melbourne: Curriculum Services Unit, 1982, p. 17.
2. G. Little, 'Functions and Forms of School Language' *Australian Association for Research in Education: Conference Papers*, November, 1983.

APPENDIX 3

1. N.C. Martin *et. al.*, *Assessing compositions*. Glosgow: Blackie, 1965.
2. C. Cooper, 'Holistic evaluation of writing', in C. Cooper and L. Odell, (eds), *Evaluating writing: describing, measuring, judging*. Urbana, Illinois: N.C.T.E., 1977.

3. G. Bracewell, C. Bereiter and M. Scardamadia, 'How beginning writers succeed and fail in making arguments more convincing'. Unpublished paper. Ontario Institute for Studies in Education, 1979.
4. M. Dilena. 'A senior literacy curriculum: an outline of possibilities', *Opinion*, 1983, 12, 3, 3–17.
5. C. Cooper, 'Holistic evaluation of writing'.

Index